END

MW00811613

This practical gem's facets reflect a kaleidoscope of biblical patterns for spiritual leadership. However, two of them are especially conspicuous: personal example and public exposition. These characteristics are biblically in accord with the same areas of responsibility and accountability laid upon Timothy and Titus (e.g., 1 Tim 4:12–16) by Paul. And, of course, Paul himself exemplified them (e.g., Acts 20:17–38), since he followed the model of the Master. Wragg also makes it clear theologically that spiritual influence is God-given, thereby challenging the would-be leader with the need for lifelong prayer for and pursuit of humility. This circumscribing attribute is the atmosphere in which all the other characteristics of biblical leadership breathe and grow.

Since the essentiality of humility is woven into all the pages of *Courageous Churchmen*, as you read be prepared to be challenged by the implications of Jesus' words to His disciples who were vying for superior positions of leadership: "If anyone would be first, he must be last of all and servant of all" (Mark 9:35). If your desire is to be a spiritual leader as defined by Scripture, you cannot afford not to read this doctrinally accurate and exceedingly practical volume.

George J. Zemek, Th.D., Academic Dean,
The Expositors Seminary

Unlike many resources on spiritual leadership, *Courageous Churchmen* is both biblically sound and immensely practical. No other book has been so instrumental in helping me grow in my faithfulness as a man of God. I can't recommend it more highly.

Matt Waymeyer, Pastor of Discipleship,
Grace Immanuel Bible Church, Jupiter, Florida,
Faculty Member, The Expositors Seminary

Having known Pastor Jerry Wragg for thirty years—including having served alongside him in pastoral ministry for several of those years—I have been enormously impacted by his keen and effective spiritual influence. As I read what Dr. Wragg has written, I couldn't help but think, "Yes! Yes! And the man who is again teaching me about these excellent biblical principles carefully lives out what he's preaching! He's truly influenced me from virtually every perspective spoken about in this book! How grateful I am for this man of God!" In addition to Jerry's influence upon my own life, I've also seen the impact he's had upon the lives of many others, especially a number of young men who are either already in ministry or who are shortly headed that way.

As far as the actual content of the book is concerned, you hold in your hand a penetrating, compelling analysis of what really constitutes lasting spiritual leadership and influence upon the lives of others. Keying into such areas of leadership as modeling, humility, integrity, stamina, gifts, criticism, conflict, and watchfulness, as well as identifying and addressing these same areas in future potential leaders, and then finally seeking to tie up loose ends with respect to various other leadership dimensions, the book delivers well on its title and theme. Using a myriad of biblical examples from which to derive his principles, with a veritable feast of good quotes on these leadership subjects from other notable writers, and with his own clear, sharp, pithy writing style, Pastor Wragg has done the body of Christ a wonderful service. I, for one, applaud his efforts in both writing on and living out what it means to be a courageous churchman. If you read what he has written on this vital topic, I believe you too will thank God for his efforts and will in turn be impacted in how to lead and influence others.

Lance Quinn, Senior Pastor,
Bethany Church on the Hill,
Thousand Oaks, California

No one has been more helpful to me through the years on the subject of leadership than Jerry Wragg, whether through personal conversation, his preaching, or his modeling of biblical principles. This book captures in print many of the life-changing lessons I've learned from him. But open its pages with fear and trembling. Wragg is a skillful heart surgeon, and his scalpel cuts deep (would we have it any other way?). Whether you are mature or a novice in Christian ministry, this book is just what you need to continue to advance in your leadership as you serve our great Leader, the Lord Jesus Christ.

Dr. Joel James, Pastor-Teacher,
Grace Fellowship,
Pretoria, South Africa

Leadership is more easily discussed and described than exemplified and developed. *Courageous Churchmen* is the connective tissue between theory and practice. This book integrates character and skill, formality and informality, and deliberate and consequential dimensions of leadership. Drawing from careful exegesis and rich pastoral experience, Jerry Wragg has produced a one-volume curriculum for any leader in Christ's church. This book not only aids in understanding spiritual leadership, it is also a sure guide for becoming a more effective servant for the Savior.

Dr. Rick Holland, Senior Pastor,
Mission Road Bible Church, Prairie Village, Kansas,
Faculty Member, The Expositors Seminary

Courageous Churchmen is far from the cluttered landscape of pop-culture's volumes depicting and promoting CEO-style management for God's leaders in the church. Jerry plumbs the depths and from the Word of God masterfully develops the absolutely essential need of a vibrant inner life for truly effective spiritual leadership. *Courageous Churchmen* is reminiscent of the works written by the godly Puritan "doctors of the soul" of centuries ago, but with keen insight and commentary on contemporary culture. This book, born in the fertile soil of pastoral leadership and deep study of the Bible, has the sweet smell of Christ on every page. The chapter "Strength Sheathed in Meekness" is worth the price of the book alone. Incisively challenging, yet warmly affirming, *Courageous Churchmen* is a vital addition to the small number of books on leadership really worth owning.

Stephen Lonetti, Pastor for Preaching and Vision,
Beacon of Hope Church,
Saint Paul, Minnesota

Of all the pastors I've known during the privileged thirty-four years I've spent in pastoral ministry, I don't know of anyone who takes spiritual leadership more seriously than Dr. Wragg. I've watched his life and ministry, I've experienced and witnessed his influence on others in pastoral matters, and I can't give a higher recommendation concerning his biblical and practical wisdom and faithfulness in pastoral ministry. *Courageous Churchmen* is the unpacking of years biblical knowledge and practical experience in spiritual leadership. I am thankful for the work, and I wish that every pastor would read it.

Richard Caldwell, Pastor-Teacher,
Founders Baptist Church, Spring, Texas,
Faculty Member, The Expositors Seminary

Jerry Wragg has hit the proverbial nail on the head. Such a topic could not be taught by a better man. I revel in the fact that this work is now in print as I am able to personally testify of Wragg's knowledge and practice of this material in my own life for many years. In a world where the topic is in vogue and yet the need still so clearly seen, Wragg points the compass toward true north and shows us how to think about and practice leadership. I cannot commend the man or the message strongly enough.

Eric Bancroft, Senior Pastor,
Castleview Baptist Church,
Indianapolis, Indiana

In a day in which the understanding of spiritual leadership has been corrupted by managerial science, shameless pragmatism, and selfish ambition, this work builds its convictions from Scripture's non-negotiable high calling of personal humility, holiness, and integrity required of every leader of Christ's church.

J. Todd Murray, Pastor of Family Ministries,
Grace Immanuel Bible Church,
Jupiter, Florida

COURAGEOUS
CHURCHMEN

LEADERS COMPELLING
ENOUGH TO FOLLOW

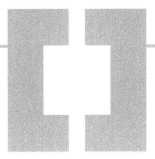

KRESS
BIBLICAL
RESOURCES

Kress Biblical Resources
The Woodlands, Texas
www.kressbiblical.com

ISBN: 978-1-934952-34-4

Unless otherwise indicated, Scripture quotations are from The Holy Bible, English Standard Version (ESV), copyright © 2001 by Crossway Bibles, a publishing ministry of Good News Publishers. Used by permission. All rights reserved.

Italics in Scripture quotations have been added by the author for emphasis.

DEDICATION

This volume is dedicated, first, to my two sons, Jordan and Aaron: your friendship is one of the highest joys of my life. Thank you both for helping me become a more Christlike leader through our constant conversations about the truth of God's Word.

Second, to my sons-in-law, Steve and Ryan: your commitment to leading your families in the fear of Christ is a grace from the Lord to our daughters.

Third, to the elders at Grace Immanuel Bible Church: thank you for praying for me and expecting me to humbly live according to the principles in this book. Your love and care is a rich grace in my life.

Fourth, to the body of Christ at Grace Immanuel Bible Church: your humble submission to the truth—despite coming through such a flawed vessel as I—continues to be an encouragement to my heart beyond what I could've asked or imagined.

CONTENTS

ACKNOWLEDGEMENTS

This revised and expanded volume has proved to be a timely source of spiritual refreshment for me. Since the original project, I've had several more years of applying these principles to the formidable challenges of leading God's people. Many ministry comrades partnered with me in the original project, and now several other fellow-laborers worked extensively to refine, clarify, and expand this current volume. I would like to express my deepest gratitude to my wife, Louise, for always urging me to greater courage in life and gospel ministry. She has been my confidante, best friend, and most faithful advocate in the challenges of leading our family and our ministry. I could not accomplish a moment of effective spiritual influence without her at my side. I am very grateful to so many who have prayed for, challenged, and encouraged me throughout this current work. My special thanks go to Joel James for his invaluable edits and many personal encouragements. I'm grateful as well for the tireless reading, exceptional organizing, and careful editing of the new material by Whitney Oxford. I'm deeply indebted to Daron Roberts for modeling what a faithful "Timothy" looks like in the training of the next generation of leaders. Also, I couldn't have completed the project without the helpful labors of our exceptional administrative assistants, Darla Orrell and Anna Scheffer. A special thanks goes to my church staff for tolerating my absences and distractedness. I'm also very grateful for the leadership team of godly elders/pastors that the Lord has placed alongside me in the grace of gospel ministry. They are ever striving to humbly live what these chapters express. I'm deeply indebted to Lance Quinn for his vital

1

input over the years and for modeling what the book presents. I am especially grateful to John MacArthur for his years of personal mentoring and his tireless example of slavery to Jesus Christ, both of which continue to richly impact my life as a shepherd and servant of God's flock. Finally, I want to offer a heart of thankfulness to the godly men and women within my family. Our ladies have continually prayed for the men of the family and expected us strive hard after Christ. The men have been learning to sheath their strength in humility and die to self that we might be more useful to the Master. May we always remain vitally linked to our courageous Savior. And thank you to our church family at Grace Immanuel Bible Church for opening your hearts wide to those whom the Lord gives us to teach and train for leadership. Thank you for graciously hosting our annual conference for pastors that they might learn to be Courageous Churchmen. And thank you for your love of the truth, your hunger for greater spiritual conviction, and your proven commitment to the biblical training of shepherds after God's own heart.

FOREWORD

Bookstores are well stocked with books on leadership, and most of them are filled with dangerously bad advice for people in positions of *spiritual* leadership.

Contemporary models of corporate and secular leadership all seem to stress things like the tricks and techniques for leveraging authority to get maximum results, how to increase one's clout, or how to cultivate a powerful image. Illustrations and explanations of leadership principles usually appeal to corporate CEOs, politicians, celebrities, or army generals as the primary models of leadership. The contemporary notion of leadership is all about dominion, fame, material success, authority, stylishness, and similar issues. The *image* of the leader is paramount. There are whole books on how to perfect a more urbane style in dress and mannerisms in order to maximize one's power over others through a subtle form of intimidation.

Jesus took the completely opposite approach to spiritual leadership. He called the Twelve to him and said, "You know that the rulers of the Gentiles lord it over them, and their great ones exercise authority over them. It shall not be so among you. But whoever would be great among you must be your servant, and whoever would be first among you must be your slave, even as the Son of Man came not to be served but to serve, and to give his life as a ransom for many" (Matt 20:25–28).

In other words, true spiritual leadership is all about service, humility, and self-sacrifice. "The greatest among you shall be your servant" (Matt 23:11).

Yes, of course, leadership is *influence*. A leader is a leader precisely because people follow him or her. But *how* the exemplary spiritual leader influences followers stands in stark contrast to the leadership style of a military commander, an earthly potentate, or a corporate suit whose whole identity as a leader is epitomized by an expensive haircut or a "power tie."

The singular model of *spiritual* leadership is Christ himself, of course. His approach to leadership was dominated by self-giving and humble service to others. When he wanted to give his disciples a lesson in leadership and leave them with the most vivid possible human archetype, he girded himself like a common household slave and washed their feet.

Christian leadership, quite frankly, is nothing like most people think, and the kinds of leaders God chooses and blesses are almost never individuals whom the world would naturally esteem as "great." Jesus himself chose fishermen and lowlifes—a ragtag collection of common laborers and nobodies—and trained them to be the apostles and pillars on whom he built his church. Service, not superiority, was the hallmark of the "style" Jesus modeled for his disciples and required of them. There's a reason why the New Testament gives church leaders the title "pastor"—literally, "shepherd"—rather than "master" or "overlord."

Infinitely more crucial than any question of style or technique is the leader's *character*. Integrity, faithfulness, love for people, a willingness to give oneself, and a host of similar virtues are the true qualifications for spiritual leadership. In fact, when the New Testament sets forth lists of qualifications for elders and deacons in the church (1 Tim 3:1–12; Titus 1:7–9), every requirement is a character quality (rather than a skill) except one: elders must be gifted to teach.

Jerry Wragg is uniquely qualified to write a book titled *Courageous Churchmen*. He is both a capable teacher and a natural leader, and is committed to Jesus' pattern of humility and self-sacrifice as the only viable model of church leadership. This book is a refreshing, readable study of what it means to be a godly leader. Since practically all Christians have a calling to leadership at one level or another (Heb 5:12), every Christian will find this book a profitable study and an encouraging, practical resource— one they will return to again and again.

Whether you are just starting to disciple others or have been a pastor for decades, I know you'll find much in this volume that will challenge and provoke, and encourage you to be more Christlike in your leadership. May the impact of this study be profound and lasting, not just for you, but for those whom you lead as well.

John MacArthur

INTRODUCTION

Ever since becoming a husband and father many years ago, I've been faced with the demands of spiritual leadership. Of course, being so young I didn't know the first thing about it, and lacked the understanding and experience to lead effectively. But life doesn't seem to care whether we're ready to lead or not, and the moment we assume responsibility for the lives of others, we're called to the task. Seasoned or just beginning, we're expected to make difficult decisions, wisely navigate ethical dilemmas, protect and provide for others, model godly character, and remain steadfast for as long as we live. If that weren't frightening enough, all our blunders can have a negative impact—not just on our lives, but also on those we lead. Becoming a wise and skilled leader simply takes time—a lifetime in fact.

My early years were filled with many mistakes, a few bright spots, and an increasingly desperate desire to learn what the essentials of strong, faithful leadership look like. There was growing in me a deep burden for my own sons. I have seen the wreckage of families without godly leadership, and I've been on the counseling end of stunned and grieving churches dealing with the aftermath of unfaithful shepherds. What would I teach my boys about this daunting responsibility, and more urgently, how would I be able to faithfully live it in front of them? Good intentions simply aren't enough to create a lasting legacy! Godly, faithful leaders are men of strong conviction and noble character, virtues intensely pursued and steadily cultivated. They are men who understand that spiritual influence ultimately comes from God alone, and that nothing of eternal value can be accomplished without His favor.

They understand that business trends and pop-cultural opinions come and go, but the heart of a truly effective leader is uncompromising, unwavering in his spiritual life. We desperately need exemplary leaders who won't flinch when tempted by the lure of power and human praise. We need men who refuse to capitulate to every fad and fashionable leadership technique our culture offers up. Fathers must train their sons, pastors must train their flocks, and leaders must pass the baton to faithful disciples "who will be able to teach others also" (2 Tim 2:2). Where such essentials are grossly neglected, families and churches spiral downward, leaving future generations starving for the truth and without hope.

Obviously, leadership is one of those subjects that no one book can cover completely. There are wide-angle approaches covering the broadest categories, and more narrowly-focused treatments dealing with one or two specific issues. Leadership is sometimes described in management terms—a sort of business CEO model—and other times viewed through a more relational lens where interpersonal skills are considered highly critical for effectiveness. The chasm between perspectives can leave any aspiring leader confused and overwhelmed. How do we boil it down? Is there a way to understand the core essentials of spiritual leadership that allows application across the spectrum of the Christian life? There may be. I'm not sure this volume accomplishes the goal, but it represents my feeble attempt at articulating what it takes to become a Courageous Churchman.

I'm convinced that at the heart of an ability to influence others is a compelling life of fearless conviction and a transcendent, divine message. A man who lives in the fear of God and boldly speaks His truth to the world is the kind of leader God promises to bless (Isa 66:2). Where are such men today? The world's model leader is someone of financial means, political power, or social popularity, but these shouldn't be premium qualities in the church. Yet, evangelicalism has suffered four decades of insipid leaders who fear men and compromise truth. It's no wonder that so many books on leadership can't put their finger on the

dynamics of spiritual influence. We must get back to the biblical principles which God says will make us useful to the Master
(2 Tim 2:21). When a man's life manifests a righteous character
and the spiritual convictions which cannot be shaken, others can't
resist following such moral strength. Moreover, the culture desperately looks in vain for answers to life's most difficult problems,
and a man of profound wisdom is hard to deny. Strong and effective spiritual leaders are men who tirelessly strive to forge godly
habits. They speak truth and take stands without wavering. Such
men of influence tremble at God's Word rather than cater to the
culture. The challenges of godly leadership are formidable and
the dangers sobering, but God has provided all that we need to
become strong instruments in His hand. May God grant us the
grace to practice the principles in these chapters.

PART

1

THE DYNAMICS
OF LEADERSHIP

A LIFE WORTH
FOLLOWING

What is it that compels a group of people to follow the leadership and vision of one person? Why are the insights and pursuits of certain individuals more persuasive than others? What is "influence," and what are the dynamics that make it pivotal for leadership? These are honest questions that face every aspiring leader tasked with a great cause and the responsibility of mobilizing others to achieve it. Simply defined, influence is a power affecting a person, thing, or event.[1] With reference to leadership, it is the ability to impact, persuade, and convince others to follow a particular course and achieve named objectives. Influence may be reduced to two concepts: (1) living a life compelling enough to follow; (2) communicating a message compelling enough to hear. Those who need leadership will enjoy optimum benefit from leaders whose lives are a model to emulate, and whose profound insights transcend the ordinary.

In the case of those who lead spiritually, the stakes are of the highest kind because the spiritual maturity of God's people hangs in the balance. At every level of the Christian life there is

---

1   *Webster's II New Riverside University Dictionary*, s.v. "Influence," 627.

the potential to influence others for their good or to their detriment. Leaders bear a profound burden knowing that people have pledged their loyalty and often will follow blindly. Of this sobering reality, Henry and Richard Blackaby caution that

> With influence comes a tremendous responsibility. Therefore a weighty issue for leaders is their management of influence. When people trust their leaders, they give them the benefit of the doubt. Such power can seduce unwary leaders into using people to achieve their own selfish ends. Influence used for selfish purposes is nothing more than crass manipulation and political scheming. People need to know their leaders have their best interest at heart.[2]

The apostle James captured the essence of this stewardship with a solemn warning: "Not many of you should become teachers, my brothers, for you know that we who teach will be judged with greater strictness" (Jas 3:1). Tragically, in today's personality-driven culture where leaders gain influence by charisma, jet-set lifestyles, shock-speech, or anti-tradition rhetoric, the noble qualities of biblical leadership are marginalized. Leadership in the church is often plagued with confusion and beset with weaknesses that drain spiritual resources and hinder growth. Over the years, I've observed some common flaws that rob the church of her vitality and effectiveness.

- Churches become discontent over dwindling numbers, strained budgets, increased persecution, academic ridicule, and cultural marginalization. Frantic leaders rush to seminars and bookshelves trying to stop the decline in

---

2   Henry T. and Richard Blackaby, *Spiritual Leadership* (Nashville, TN: Broadman & Holman, 2001), 175.

"effectiveness." Such promising resources have become the regimen of an evangelical church that has made an idol out of "the impact we used to have."

- Many figureheads rely heavily on personal charisma and natural talent as the strength of their influence. They tend to "wing it" in the face of real spiritual needs, often giving superficial counsel with little biblical foundation.

- Leadership positions are frequently occupied by men who crave the praise of others. They lead by opportunism and self-promotion for the purpose of receiving attention.

- Power struggles and politicking are the only style of leadership some churches have ever known. Sinfully fearful and insecure leaders create an environment of suspicion and distrust because they cannot risk letting others see their weaknesses. Such men become hidden, inflexible, and uncomfortable in the presence of gifted peers.

- Ministries are sometimes headed up by men who quickly run from conflict at any cost. Instead of courage, they are ruled by self-preservation and personal comfort. Whenever conflict arises, truth and doctrinal convictions are sacrificed on the altar of relational harmony. The church flounders under the leadership of a hireling.

- With today's postmodern generation, influence is obtained by speaking out against anything that represents a rigid, absolute standard for living. A new breed of church leaders has gained prominence by identifying with a disillusioned youth pop-culture that denies the existence of objective truth. For these churches, tradition is the new enemy and social outreach is "the Jesus way of life." Leadership in these ministries requires almost no formal theological training, and a penchant for raw, low-brow behavior and speech.

Increasingly, the secular culture reduces leadership to what sells in the public arena. And the church has fared no better, riding the wave of cultural popularity as long as she can until the next paradigm shift in the popular opinion polls. Is this what influence should look like? How are leaders made? Does someone become a leader simply because others follow? And what about the long-term spiritual fallout? Will today's spiritual influencers be around in thirty years to take responsibility for what they've produced? These are serious questions that deserve biblical answers. The church's leadership crisis won't be solved with another strategy meeting or the total abandonment of our heritage. I believe we must return to the throne of grace and plead with God to raise up a mighty generation of churchmen who will lead His people out of the cultural desert and into abundance.

THE AGE OF PRAGMATISM AND GIMMICKS

The reality is that true spiritual influence is a *gift from God* and cannot be manufactured by men. Any philosophy of leadership or influence which trades the supernatural work of God for man-made imitations will eventually degenerate into trite solutions and pragmatic goals. Sadly, ours is a generation of new leaders who believe that influence depends on human innovations and gimmicks. They have concluded that God's Word has somehow left out some of the most crucial keys to dynamic spiritual influence. It is a widely accepted notion that since the culture is resistant to the truth claims of Scripture we must shift our emphasis, immerse ourselves in the lifestyle of the culture, and offer a more palatable message. Whatever happened to the unashamed proclamation of truth in the plain language of the Bible? God's revelation offers the only true clarity available where humanity is concerned.

When the apostle Paul arrived in Corinth his message and preaching "were not in plausible words of wisdom, but in demonstration of the Spirit and of power" (1 Cor 2:4). He knew the grave danger of man's tendency to trust in eloquent arguments and lofty reasoning. There was no doubting Paul's passion to see God move mightily in the hearts of sinners, but he shuddered to think that someone might find his speech more attractive than truth. More than on mere oratory skill, he wanted the Corinthians' faith to rest exclusively "in the power of God" (1 Cor 2:5). Reaching their ears with the saving gospel of Jesus Christ was Paul's awesome privilege and responsibility, but reaching their hearts with the gospel's life-giving power is God's sovereign joy!

Today's emphasis on packaging the gospel according to cultural demands doesn't beautify truth, but dresses up error. Divine truth itself does not change, and until sinners stop demanding a different message and face God on His terms, they can never know saving grace. A lost man is incapable of seeing his true spiritual need on his own. That is why the Scriptures are so clear about human depravity and our desperate need for the convicting work of the Spirit (John 3:3; 1 Cor 2:12–14). Before conversion I had a host of religious notions but no clue as to real spiritual realities (e.g., holiness, sin, judgment, saving grace). No unbeliever can determine what kind of message can "reach" his culture. That's like asking a fish to describe his surroundings and wondering why it doesn't mention the water!

In the progressive city of Thessalonica, the penetrating, unambiguous message of a crucified and risen Christ descended upon a group of culturally relevant idol-worshippers like a military invasion, powerfully taking their hearts captive to the truth. Did the missionaries bring a road show of clever speeches or social rhetoric? Not at all! Here's how Paul described what happened: "And we also thank God constantly for this, that when you received the word of God, which you heart from us, you accepted it not as the word of men but as what it really is, the word of God, which is at work in you believers" (1 Thess 2:13).

These first-time hearers of the good news welcomed the Word of God *by faith*, and their eyes were opened. They instantly knew, by divine grace, that this was no cleverly staged performance designed to make truth "acceptable." The straightforward truth of Scripture is able both to open blind eyes and to transform the heart (Ps 19:7–11). Supernatural discernment comes from a mind saturated with truth (Ps 119:97–104). It brings clarity to flaws, liberates the conscience (Jas 1:25), uncovers the deepest issues of the inner man (Heb 4:12), and fully equips the believer for a life of pleasing God (2 Tim 3:16–17). Many leadership models today have utterly abandoned a simple trust in the work of the Holy Spirit to bring effective spiritual influence, and the results have been disastrous! As Phillip R. Johnson contends,

> This is one of the real deficiencies in this generation of evangelicals. We don't have enough faith in the power of God's Word to penetrate a hardened heart. [We] think it's necessary to have … entertainment ("pre-evangelism") to soften people up and prepare them to receive the Word. And in most cases those who opt for such a strategy *never do* get around to declaring the Word of God with any kind of boldness. The idea is to find some activity or technique that entertains people and tries to make them friendly to Christianity while carefully avoiding the risk of confronting them with the truth of Scripture—as if something besides the Word of God might be *more* effective … at penetrating their hearts. That is sheer folly, and all the emphasis given to such gimmickry these days is a tremendous waste of time and energy. *Nothing* is more penetrating and more effective in reaching sin-hardened hearts than the pure and unadulterated Word of God. All our human techniques and ingenuity are like

dull plastic butter knives compared to the Word of God, which is "sharper than any two-edged sword."[3]

Evangelism and "outreach" is now the subject of strategy meetings, think-tanks, and "culturally relevant conversations" rather than the inflamed result of biblically "equip[ing] the saints for the work of ministry" (Eph 4:12). The Christian culture has been unwittingly sitting under a steady diet of poor Bible teaching and lazy shepherding, leaving God's people without discernment in the most basic Christian doctrines. Churches abound in theological and religious clichés about cultural impact and relevance, but they lack the divine content. With this growing biblical illiteracy has come the inevitable man-centered perspective on true sanctification. The lofty grandeur of knowing resurrection power has been replaced by the idols of emotional, psychological, and communal wholeness. Sanctification is seen as the result of having God and others meet our needs. The suffering and rejection of Christ's cross, far from atoning for sin, is championed as an example of humanitarian love and compassion. Over time, true believers weaken under such skeletal teaching, becoming enslaved to sin and weighed down with guilt. Discouraged, they begin to distrust the Scriptures and lose all confidence (and interest) in its power to dramatically change a life.

How did the church become so diseased? It's simple: the contemporary church has been hemorrhaging truth and pumping in self-worship at such a rate that unbelievers, longing to drown their guilt and angst in religious renewal, find church-going a welcome and *undemanding* refuge. And why shouldn't they? The average fad-soaked postmodern worship service has just enough morality to soothe the secular conscience, and enough worldliness to leave

---

3   Phillip Johnson, "What's Wrong with Jumping on and off the Fad Wagons?" July 28, 2005, http://phillipjohnson.blogspot.com/2005/07/whats-wrong-with-jumping-on-and-off.html; emphasis original.

superficial Christians feeling right at home. Leaders who make a habit of relying on natural talent, glibness, cutting edge marketing, or raw worldliness create a façade of apparent progress, but the results over time reveal a glaring lack of depth. Churches find they've been dragged down every trendy path as imprudent leaders chase the latest trends that promise exciting ministry influence. It is the severest tragedy, as John MacArthur asserts, "when the church's immature believers are among its most influential teachers and leaders."[4] Rather than a deeper walk with Christ, the result is a congregation pooling in a cul-de-sac of stagnant, ingrown, and carnal ministry. Such is the tragic legacy of man's attempt at influence on his own terms. Without the regular proclamation of the living and abiding Word of God and the convicting power of the Holy Spirit, true spiritual influence dries up and the body of Christ is starved of real sustenance.

It's no secret that the church-hopping patterns of many evangelicals are a direct result of the superficial ministry philosophy of their leaders. Every time I've addressed a group of Christians on the importance of committing to serve and use their gifts in one local church, invariably a flurry of challenges is launched by some who see no problem with "shopping" the ministry merchandise that's available. Worse, the leadership of many pragmatic ministries encourages this cafeteria-style approach to body life. The biblical privileges of shepherding, accountability, discipleship, holy living, and obeying the "one anothers" seem to have escaped today's ministry designers. This environment may be preferable to the previously "un-churched" or disenfranchised postmodern masses, but it will not do for those who begin to understand their need for the truth. True believers under repeated malnourishment will eventually seek food for their souls, often landing in some small fellowship where powerful preaching is a feast by comparison.

---

4   John MacArthur, *The Power of Integrity* (Wheaton, IL: Crossway Books, 1997), 30.

LEADERS ARE DIVINELY APPOINTED

We need leaders who put their confidence in the Word of God alone for the growth of God's people. The Lord Jesus Christ said He would build His church (Matt 16:18), and we cannot sit idle while the sheep are ravaged by ministry leaders who've resigned their responsibility to trust in "the living and abiding word of God" (1 Pet 1:23). Leaders of many stripes come and go, but those who, by the power of the Holy Spirit, live a compelling life of faithfulness and speak for the living God will have a uniquely blessed influence. Derek Prime's clarity here is helpful: "That a man should be 'full of the Holy Spirit' is the major requirement for Christian leadership, and an essential difference from all other kinds."[5] All the natural talent and savoir-faire admired by men cannot produce a spiritually dynamic, biblically wise, and unswervingly steadfast spiritual leader. Such men are raised up, tested, and sustained by God's grace and appointment. Prime goes on to say,

> Christian leaders are essentially Christ-made. While they possess natural abilities it is the Holy Spirit who enables them to use them to the benefit of the church. He is Christ's gift to them ... Christ makes and provides leaders for His church... Leaders in other spheres may sometimes describe themselves as self-made or duly qualified because of examinations passed, but not so Christian leaders.[6]

When we are thoroughly convinced of our own inadequacy, our usefulness to God is accelerated. Every great spiritual leader

---

5   Derek Prime, *A Christian's Guide to Leadership for the Whole Church* (Faverdale North, Darlington, England: Evangelical Press, 2005), 28.

6   Ibid., 29–30.

must readily admit the "strange paradox"[7] of being called by God to lead others where only God can blaze a trail. This daunting task should be met with a healthy dose of apprehension, which curbs our natural delight in being overconfident. If no such hesitation is readily apparent, the leadership role should be avoided. A. W. Tozer's oft-quoted excerpt on leadership ambition is a strong word in this regard:

> A true and safe leader is likely to be one who has no desire to lead, but is forced into a position of leadership by the inward pressure of the Holy Spirit and the press of the external situation. Such were Moses and David and the Old Testament prophets. I think there was hardly a great leader from Paul to the present day but was drafted by the Holy Spirit for the task, and commissioned by the Lord of the Church to fill a position he had little heart for. I believe it might be accepted as a fairly reliable rule of thumb that the man who is ambitious to lead is disqualified as a leader. The true leader will have no desire to lord it over God's heritage, but will be humble, gentle, self-sacrificing and altogether as ready to follow as to lead, when the Spirit makes it clear that a wiser and more gifted man than himself has appeared.[8]

Like the apostle Paul, the dependent leader openly declares to friend and foe that his "sufficiency is from God" (2 Cor 3:5) and that no mortal has the inherent spiritual capacity to come to another's aid. Only those whom "God has made a leader"[9] are truly competent for the task. The ancient people of God worshiped around

---

7   Henry T. and Richard Blackaby, *Spiritual Leadership*, 21.

8   A. W. Tozer, *The Warfare of the Spirit* (Camp Hill, PA: Wing Spread Publishers, 2006), 175.

9   John MacArthur, Jr., *The Book on Leadership* (Nashville, TN: Nelson Books, 2004), 89.

such themes, gratefully praising God for His sovereign power over dominion and influence. In Psalm 75:6–7, the rise to exaltation does not come from human advancement, innovation, or might, but from an all-wise God whose right to rule has no equal. He alone "executes judgment, putting down one and lifting up another." Eternal influence, therefore, must line up with His purposes, for without divine approval and power man can accomplish nothing.

Moreover, it is the *godly character* of a leader that determines the level of beneficial and long-term influence in spiritual matters. If others are to be effectively launched in a Godward direction a leader must ignite the fuel of his own intimate walk with Jesus Christ! Those who center the leadership task on street-savvy and popular opinion are missing the essence of spiritual influence. The goal of all spiritual privilege is the display and magnification of God's glory (1 Cor 10:31); therefore, the measure of effective leadership is grounded in the progress of sanctification, first for leaders, then for those they influence. In other words, it is *only* the character and faithful labor of leaders that ultimately distinguishes their service. Other practical helps and unique talents may offer logistical benefit but will accomplish nothing of lasting impact.

> *Gracious Lord, rescue me from the error of attributing my influence to my own innovation, people skills, or inspirational techniques. May I always remember that leadership is a privilege given by You, and it mustn't be squandered in carnal aspirations or the latest crowd-pleasing gimmicks. Help me to rightly sense the weight of gospel ministry, to long for Your perfect leadership and guidance, and to battle hard against the desire for worldly success. Amen.*

GOD LOOKS ON
THE HEART

While leadership resources abound in talk of personal charisma and professionalism, the New Testament anchors spiritual influence exclusively to a godly life! The great Charles Haddon Spurgeon once said, "Let us aspire to saintliness of spirit and character. I am persuaded that the greatest power we can get over our fellow-men is the power which comes of consecration and holiness."[1] Indeed, where spiritual virtue is highest, our influence yields eternal fruit and not some earthly substitute. The *power* of our influence grows out of the soil of a deep devotion to Christ. In 2 Timothy 2:21, the apostle Paul ties spiritual usefulness *directly* to the absence of wickedness. He states that God's leaders will have eternal impact when they are "vessel[s] for honorable use, set apart as holy, useful to the master of the house, ready for every good work." To put it succinctly, usefulness is next to godliness!

Some time ago, while perusing the bookstore at a conference for church leaders, I noticed a new book on biblical counseling. Excited, I picked it up, hoping to gain another worthy resource for our ministry. Recognizing one of the authors, however, I quickly

---

1   C. H. Spurgeon, *An All-Round Ministry*, (1900; repr., Edinburgh, Banner of Truth, 2000), 245.

put the volume back on the shelf with no further interest, remembering that his moral life was riddled with multiple affairs. I was further shocked to find this same man teaching at a Christian university, seemingly without consequence. Why is it that we've allowed men to speak into the life of the church in spite of their reproachable conduct? Is it because we cannot live without their instruction? Are they so gifted that we believe it irresponsible not to give them a platform? Spiritual credibility springs from a holy and pure life. Righteousness may not get the popular vote, but it should have no rivals in the preparation of an effective leader. From the pulpit to the pew nothing is more stabilizing, more admirable, more compelling among the leadership qualifications than our personal holiness.

REALITY MINISTRY AND THE ABSENCE OF SHAME

There is much confusion today being caused by some evangelical leaders who tell us that if we're ever going to reach the next generation, we must totally immerse ourselves in the unholy elements of the sub-culture around us. We're told that the fleshly passions, worldly practices, sensual interests, and sexually explicit speech of lost people shouldn't be a barrier to the gospel. They claim that if we are truly "missional-minded," we should wholeheartedly engage in such behavior, thereby letting unbelievers know that we're just like them in every way—that character transformation and holy living are not essential to truly knowing Jesus! Those who vigorously promote this idea have brought these elements into the leadership of the church. Contrary to what the New Testament says about pastors and shepherds being "above reproach" in their moral character (1 Tim 3:2), today's "relevance" gurus think nothing of standing before a congregation in a worship service and smothering the sermon in salacious speech and explicit vulgarity for the sake of a laugh!

What's worse is that entire congregations seem invigorated by the most graphic content possible, as though regularly violating their basic sense of propriety will have no serious effect on discernment! Perhaps I'm naïve, but if the saving gospel of Christ's forgiveness is the *true* goal of evangelism, wouldn't we take great pains to demonstrate its power over sin, carnal lust, and temptation? What does it mean to *reach* a lost soul for Jesus Christ if their lostness is merely that they haven't yet added Jesus to their already immoral lifestyle? Are we offering unbelievers a gospel that *actually* frees them from idolatry and impurity, or one that simply redefines such destructive bondage as "normal" and therefore trivial to God's work of salvation? As I wrote to one concerned friend, "Welcome to the wacky world of post-evangelical church life!"

These trends are far from a sign that the church has come of age in its ability to impact the world for Jesus Christ. The truth is that such behavior signals a wholesale abandonment of the Christian disciplines necessary for true sanctification. The personal study of God's Word and sitting under powerful preaching are *supernatural* means by which the Spirit transforms our mind and character. Giving, prayer, meditation, corporate worship, evangelism, spiritual service, and fasting all play a vital role in our becoming holy. Many of today's young evangelical leaders are the product, not of sanctifying disciplines, but of our culture's obsession with shameless sensuality. The pursuit of personal holiness doesn't even appear on their radar. They seem energized by sensuality rather than becoming vessels "set apart as holy, useful to the master … ready for every good work" (2 Tim 2:21).

I see a parallel between the raw, out-in-the-open, undignified antics of post-evangelical ministry, and the normalizing of reality TV, where the shameless airing of human "dirty laundry" is no longer shocking. It's no secret that our culture and the media are consumed with the idea that stripping people of their dignity on national television is great entertainment. When severe suffering, coarse emotion, gross exposure, and even humiliation before a mocking crowd launches prime-time ratings through the roof, something is dreadfully wrong! We have reality shows that are actually defined by putting a camera into the private worlds of troubled and very afflicted people, capturing all the undignified behavior and vulgarity, while viewers relax with chips and soda for an evening of raw entertainment. Even the on-screen participants seem to glory in flaunting their trashed lives in front of a watching world. Our society readily forks over millions of dollars to watch movies that glorify immature, destructive exploits, all without the slightest hint of shame. Such entertainment has a *dumbing-down* effect on our sensibilities and consciences. The church is suffering from overexposure to these things, and Christians are losing their ability to discern between good and evil (1 Thess 5:21; Heb 5:14). All this lowbrow, prime-time sensuality results in a new church environment where the lowest common spiritual character is deemed "normal" for believers. Anyone striving to be holy is quickly labeled "irrelevant," because, after all, "no real Christian today can live like that!" Thomas Murphy, in his classic work, *Pastoral Theology*, pointedly spoke of the power of godly moral character with the following challenge to future leaders:

> It is beyond all question that this eminent piety is before everything else in preparation for the duties of the sacred office. It is before talents, or learning, or study, or favorable circumstances, or skill in working, or power in sermonizing. It is needed to give character and tone and strength to all these, and to every other part of the work. Without this elevated spirituality nothing else will be of much account in producing a permanent and satisfactory ministry. All else will be like erecting a building without a foundation ... Oh that at the very beginning this could be deeply impressed upon the hearts of young ministers! ... Without it success in the holy office is not to be expected.[2]

2   Thomas Murphy, *Pastoral Theology* (Audubon, NJ: Old Paths Publications, 1996), 38.

Without the fervent pursuit of godliness, preaching loses all authority, discipleship becomes cold duty, and prayer is hypocrisy.

"FASHIONABLE" LEADERS

When spiritual influence is driven, not by character first, but by the "curb appeal" of popular trends and superficial attractiveness, God's people suffer for generations! First Samuel records the destructive trail of Israel's failure to long for a leader after God's own heart when choosing a king. Before Saul's appointment as monarch, the people had looked exclusively *to the Lord* for protection, guidance, and preservation through the leadership of Samuel, God's choice servant of indisputable character (1 Sam 7:8–12). But as they became fearful of men and enamored with the apparent security and power of other nations, their hearts plunged into arrogant presumption and they demanded a leader *of their own choosing.* Samuel warned Israel of such foolish thinking, but they quickly dismissed God's valuation of kingly readiness and sought a man after the fashion of the day. They would not risk following a primarily spiritual leader if it meant a greater vulnerability to their enemies. After all, exclusive dependence upon God had made life very difficult, and the people were forsaking their confidence in God's protection and provision. Character would eventually make Israel's list of desired qualities, but the top candidate must first measure up to the cultural ideal. Their main concern was to find an internationally respectable monarch in order to blend in with the surrounding cultures—"a king to judge us like all the nations" (1 Sam 8:5). In their pride they had been envious of other nations whose leaders were regarded as the standard of powerful influence and skill.

This is not unlike today's notion that strong leadership is the ability to attract the attention of the mob and wield its influence. Crowds may be mobilized, managed, and inspired to achieve a goal, but without the rudder of moral virtue people are dashed on the rocks of pride and turf battles. This same kind of pragmatism is the fatal flaw of the "emergent church," whose philosophy of ministry calls for moral tolerance within a doctrinally eclectic "community." No matter how accepting and communal they become, such efforts "are of no value in stopping the indulgence of the flesh" (Col 2:23), and the inevitable result is widespread carnality. If we amass achievements without forging the necessary moral fiber to bear the responsibility, we cannot keep our hearts from self-deception.

Apart from the grace of God, none of us are formidable enough to match the deceptive bent of our own hearts, let alone the subtle schemes of the evil one. Speaking of his own vulnerability in this regard, the apostle Paul, arguably one of the greatest spiritual leaders in history, wrote, "Because of the surpassing greatness of the revelations [I've been given], for this reason, to keep me from exalting myself, there was given to me a thorn in the flesh" (2 Cor 12:7, NASB). God uses severe pressure and tribulation to crucify the sinful tendencies in leaders who've been privileged with tremendous influence. In spite of grand accomplishments and a large following, a leader without character is just another image, a cultural icon for the moment that is sure to crash and burn, replaced by tomorrow's new and improved version. Henry and Richard Blackaby's observation is on target:

> It has never been easier to create the image of a leader than it is today. In contemporary society, someone who writes a book or earns a doctorate is immediately labeled as an expert. Professional consultants provide "reputation management" for aspiring leaders to create the perception that they are genuinely qualified to lead. With the right kind of help, people can generate a lot of hype, but they are really only pseudo leaders. They have image but no substance.[3]

---

3   Henry T. and Richard Blackaby, *Spiritual Leadership*, 187.

Painfully, Israel's "image" of leadership didn't end with the desire to mimic the hierarchy of other nations. They also demanded an intimidating figurehead with political and military savvy who would ensure national security and economic comfort. "There shall be a king over us ... that our king may ... go out before us and fight our battles" (1 Sam 8:19–20). If that weren't enough, when God finally granted their desire for a king, they couldn't contain their excitement over Saul's physical stature (1 Sam 10:24). Their notion of qualified leadership had plummeted to an all-time, superficial low! Popular opinion, social comfort, and outward appearance were the chief considerations for the nation's top man. The rebellious blunder proved devastating for the people of God. Saul's rule began in victory under God's patient favor, but ended in half-hearted obedience, feigned worship, and severe chastening of the nation. His fear of man led him to offer dishonorable worship (1 Sam 13:8–13); his cowardice and self-preservation caused him to deal lightly with sin (1 Sam 14:32–35); and a final act of spiritual treason brought his reign to a bitter end (1 Sam 15:1–33).

God's closing indictment of Israel's view of leadership came at the anointing of the young, inexperienced, and unproven son of Jesse, a shepherd boy without rank, powerful personality, or distinction: "Do not look at his [David's brother Eliab] appearance or on the height of his stature, because I have rejected him. For the LORD sees not as man sees: man looks on the outward appearance, but the LORD looks on the heart" (1 Sam 16:7). None of David's brothers passed the heart test, fearing God above all. When the unassuming young shepherd boy entered the hallowed place of consecration, God affirmed the lad as His choice to lead the people (1 Sam 16:12).

It is *the heart* in relationship to God that makes us useful in spiritual leadership. The greatest damage occurs in the lives of others when we assume that power and position will make up for a lifestyle lacking in moral uprightness.[4] Anyone desiring the burden and privilege of spiritual influence must pass the test of character before God's maximum blessing can be enjoyed. While there are a number of virtues that merit our attention, the next twelve will examine *particular qualities* that give rise to all others and should therefore crown every spiritual leader's ministry.

> *Heavenly Father, I know that You see all things, and that there is nothing hidden from Your sight. Keep my heart from becoming enamored with outward appearances and vain attractions. Your greatest delight is to see truth permeate my heart and mind. May I never doubt Your leadership, but regularly subject my notions of success to Your Word. Amen.*

---

4   Larry J. Michael, *Spurgeon on Leadership* (Grand Rapids, MI: Kregel Publications, 2003), 75.

3

STRENGTH SHEATHED
IN MEEKNESS

Robert Chapman, pastor for many years at Ebenezer Chapel, Barnstaple, England, was widely regarded as a man of extraordinary patience and love for others. His selfless ministry to the struggling saints at the small chapel was born of sober humility and an acute sense of his own unworthiness. For Chapman, the godly character of a leader was measured primarily by the depth of his humble dependence upon God:

> The Servant of the Lord Jesus must be instant in season and out of season, knowing that he is the Lord's messenger to everyone with whom he has to do, and *ever learning of the Lord*; seeing that he is to be continually ministering to others, he must be receiving fresh supplies from the God of all grace through all channels … seeking in every way to magnify Christ and abase the creature.[1]

---

1   Robert L. Peterson, *Robert Chapman, A Biography* (Neptune, NJ: Loizeaux Brothers Inc., 1995), 145; emphasis added.

Evangelicalism today seems confused as to the real power behind influential leadership. Behind the walls of many organizations is a frustrated, beaten-down staff that dare not raise questions or different ideas. A self-effacing servant-leader doesn't seem to correspond with bulging crowds, inflated budgets, and renowned achievements. A humble disposition is deemed weak and therefore, says popular opinion, not conducive to motivating others toward great things.

This was illustrated to me some years ago when I was approached by two scriptwriters who were developing the storyline for Steven Spielberg's animated feature film *The Prince of Egypt*, on the life of Moses. The famed producer/director was determined to closely follow the biblical account, and wanted to hear an evangelical perspective before he went any further. After reading the preliminary script, I rather bluntly explained that they had completely missed the point of Moses' life. Their early draft of the script cast Moses as a man of extraordinary compassion who could no longer tolerate the oppression of his people at the hands of an evil empire. They could not conceive of such a powerful leader having no personal ambition or, at the very least, no humanitarian motive. For Hollywood, Israel's most influential leader simply had to be a type-A personality, a maverick, the kind of self-motivated, win-at-all-costs revolutionary with a vision to rid the world of tyranny. When I opened the Word of God to Numbers 12:3 and read of Moses' chief virtue—humility—they were speechless. "Moses' life is a story about God, not Moses," I urged. The great leader of Israel saw himself rightly, that his influential position spoke volumes about God's greatness rather than his own. When the film finally hit theaters, Moses was a mere shadow of the biblical patriarch. Far from a humble instrument for the display of God's glory, Spielberg's "prince of Egypt" was a human rights activist fighting against slavery. Ah, the power of special effects!

SECOND-CLASS VIRTUE?

Humility still receives honorable mention as a worthy trait, but in the practical chapters of many leadership resources it is a back-page subheading, frequently upstaged by "superior" qualities such as vision, team-building, innovation, or a commanding presence. Occasionally, a business strategist gets it right, listing humility among the top qualities behind leadership greatness. One of today's prized manuals on turning average businesses into great competitors, *Good to Great* by Jim Collins, ranks a humble disposition among the top two qualities of the best corporate leaders in the country.[2] Collins' research of various successful companies, of course, illustrates humility from a secular framework where self-sacrifice for larger goals and conceding a dose of "good luck" are key indicators. Not surprising, however, is the practical etiquette of humility that also surfaces from his study, such as the absence of boasting, underscoring the achievements of others, and resisting public credit. Collins' work illustrates that oftentimes non-Christians more quickly apprehend the importance of meekness than those in the church. Ken Blanchard, cofounder of The Ken Blanchard Companies, which helps businesses learn to lead effectively, crystallized the issue when he said, "The key to a servant leader's heart is humility. People with humility don't think less of themselves; they just think of themselves less."[3] But the above examples are too few, and among specific evangelical leadership resources the serious treatment of this subject is becoming scarce. The Christian community tips its hat to the nobility of meekness, but in practice pride often wins the day.

Plenty of culpability for this growing trend belongs to the now-entrenched church growth movement, which for the last few

---

2   Jim Collins, *Good to Great* (New York: Harper Collins, 2001), 22–36.

3   Ken Blanchard, "Reflections on Encourage the Heart," in *Christian Reflections on The Leadership Challenge* in Jim Kouzes and Barry Posner, eds. (San Francisco, CA: Jossey-Bass, 2004), 104.

decades has equated healthy leadership with plain old marketing know-how. In addition to the movement's abysmal depreciation of doctrine, it has spoon-fed congregations and supporters the assumption that God's people are better led by professional CEO-types rather than meek-spirited shepherds willing to get next to the sheep. Today, it is widely accepted that these two models— CEO and shepherd—are mutually exclusive. What escapes them is that the very opposite is true: clear vision and discernment are the *rewards of selfless service.* Our Lord Jesus Christ settled the matter millennia ago when He asserted, "But whoever would be great among you must be your servant" (Mark 10:43). When our leadership is self-absorbed and sinfully fearful, we are like a man whose life is beset with mirrors into which he nervously gazes to protect his own image. Resources and relationships become mere objects to be used, not for the good of others, but to advance the reputation and significance of self.

Vision and discernment flourish under a leader whose ultimate goal is larger than personal aggrandizement. A true servant-leader channels the energies and gifting of others toward worthy goals. Conversely, striving for biblical goals without a humble heart will lead to elitism, manipulation, and "every vile practice" (Jas 3:16). There is certainly nothing inherently wrong with teamwork strategies or innovative methods, but if not sheathed in meekness, such techniques become focused on moving the machinery of ministry forward at the expense of character. Our clarion call is the cultivation of humble and dependent submission. God promises to set His favorable gaze exclusively upon the leader who is "humble and contrite in spirit and trembles at [His] word" (Isa 66:2).

MEEKNESS AND LEADERSHIP: THE SEARCH FOR BALANCE

All of us at one time or another have received a word of thanks for a job well done or praise for personal qualities and talents.

But how is humility cultivated when enthusiastic followers are the leader's lot? To complicate matters, the more a leader enjoys significant achievements the more recognition and praise for his skill is sure to follow. There is even a place for publicly honoring a faithful servant, as Paul does when referring to Epaphroditus in Philippians 2:29–30: "Honor such men, for he nearly died for the work of Christ." According to Proverbs 12:8, it is quite normal for a man to be "commended according to his good sense." Striking a balance between humbly receiving a genuine compliment and seeking only the glory of Christ can be challenging.

The New Testament readily acknowledges that a leader's giftedness naturally invites more public honor: "those members of the body which we deem less honorable, on these we bestow more abundant honor ... whereas our more presentable members have no need of it. But God has so composed the body, giving more abundant honor to that member which lacked" (1 Cor 12:23–24, NASB). How does a leader process these unavoidable results without sliding into pride or taking himself too seriously? Human praise always tests the character of a leader (Prov 27:21) because it brings true motives to the surface. Ironically, asking someone to cultivate humility is a bit like asking them to think about themselves without thinking about themselves. What a seemingly impossible task! C. J. Mahaney, in his penetrating look at the subject, candidly wrote, "If I met someone presuming to have something to say about humility, automatically I'd think him unqualified to speak on the subject."[4] We have a difficult time conceiving of how to measure progress without simultaneously descending into self-focus. What's the solution?

The proper starting point begins outside of us. Humility is forged in the fires of an unmistakably clear vision of God, a biblically rich and abiding perspective of the cross, and a robust sense of man's desperate sin-condition! When confronted with

---

4   C. J. Mahaney, *Humility* (Sisters, OR: Multnomah Publishers, 2005), 13.

these realities, our deficiencies are properly magnified and successes are never allowed to take on a life of their own. A right view of God instantly brings us to the end of ourselves. When the prophet Isaiah saw the blazing holiness of Almighty God, he immediately wilted in terror, confessing, "Woe is me, for I am ruined! ... For my eyes have seen the King, the LORD of hosts" (Isa 6:5, NASB). Likewise, as we immerse ourselves in the glories of our redemption, grace is amplified and sin's vileness exposed. The apostle Peter, known for his impulsive self-trust, became instantly aware of his wretched state when he came face to face with Jesus' supernatural power over nature (Luke 5:8). Only upon honest confession of our shallow theology and the systematic forsaking of every idol of the heart can we become the leader God desires.

WE MAGNIFY HIM

On a practical level, lasting humility is nurtured when our will is broken under the reality that *we are utterly insignificant*. Psalm 8 is a good place to lay the foundation for this conviction. In a burst of adoration, David declares the unrivaled majesty of God displayed in the creation. The psalm begins and ends with praise over the *exclusive significance of God* ("how majestic is your name in all the earth!"—Ps 8:1, 9). At the song's crescendo, David is profoundly humbled by the contrast between God's vast, meticulous handiwork and man's trifling existence ("When I look at your heavens ... what is man ... ?"—Ps 8:3–4). That God would lend a thought to such inconsequential beings stirs David's heart, not toward his own significance, but to the only worthy recipient of all worship—the Creator Himself! To humbly lead others is to be convinced of one's own unimportance. John Piper's unique way of expressing this principle is poignant: "The Christian Gospel is about the 'glory of Christ,' not about me. And when it *is*—in some measure—about me, it is not about my being made much of by God, but about God mercifully enabling me to enjoy making much of him forever."[5]

In an act of stunning condescension, God uses men to carry out His purposes, even with great influence over the affairs of others. But we must be alert to the seductive power of wanting to be preeminent. When the apostle Paul was reluctantly coerced into defending his authority to lead the Corinthian church, he boldly announced, "I should have been commended by you, for in no respect was I inferior to the most eminent apostles, even though *I am a nobody*" (2 Cor 12:11, NASB). I like that! Paul's own conversion had so thoroughly embedded itself into his heart that he knew the source of all leadership opportunity. His lengthy pedigree, notable religious zeal, and years of blameless law-keeping were happily and hurriedly trashed that he might boast only in Christ (Phil 3:8)—a conviction that permeated his leadership. This was no morbid self-loathing, but a piercing grasp of how true ministry influence transpires.

Everything, from grand achievements to a seemingly trivial word of encouragement, is a privilege we don't deserve. We are mere tools in the hand of a faithful Creator to be used exclusively for His glory. Can the natural athlete rightly boast in his superior frame or competitive disposition? Does the genius justly take credit for the gift of a highly advanced intellect? Such marvels of creation are not for man's glory, but God's alone. Nothing we accomplish makes us significant at all! On the contrary, our usefulness points to God's supreme worth and preeminent significance. We sometimes behave as though our talents and gifts are indispensable to God's redemptive plan, but Scripture teaches the opposite. As Paul admonished a very gifted Corinthian congregation, "What then is Apollos? What is Paul? Servants though whom you believed, as the Lord assigned to each. I planted, Apollos watered, but God gave the growth. So neither he who plants nor

---

5   John Piper, *Seeing and Savoring Jesus Christ*, rev. ed. (Wheaton, IL: Crossway Books, 2004), 16.

he who waters is anything, but only God who gives the growth" (1 Cor 3:5–7).

The believers at Corinth were being pulled under by a tide of arrogance which required a stern reminder that giftedness and spiritual influence are given by the Lord ("What do you have that you did not receive?"—1 Cor 4:7). A leader who operates in a conscious mindset that every gift, talent, and position of influence is an undeserved privilege will not be prone to "think more highly of himself" than befits an unworthy servant (Rom 12:3, NASB). He is always grateful for the slightest assistance he's able to offer, always joyfully overwhelmed at every tiny step in the progress of those he leads. In the spirit of the missionaries who brought the gospel to Thessalonica, a humble leader never even sees his own gratitude as an adequate return "for all the joy" (1 Thess 3:9) he's experienced as the one called to lead. What an amazing perspective! Paul and his colleagues couldn't rejoice enough for having been spiritually encouraged at the growth of God's people. Their meekness was rooted in knowing that, were it not for divine grace, they too would be lost in a Christless eternity.

If we find ourselves easily irritated by immature followers, we haven't thought enough about the undeserved honor it is to serve the living God! When we neglect the formation of biblical humility, we begin to view others as hindrances to our convenience and success. Stated another way, pride leads us to view difficult people and their troubled lives as not worth our gifts, time, and energy. Instead of God's precious children, they represent obstacles to our greater accomplishments, resources to be mobilized and spent for our respectability. Humility produces just the opposite. A clear vision of God's splendor and majesty properly "downsizes" our self-assessment, resulting in a pliable, dependent disposition. Such leaders are known for their contentment, patience, consistent gratitude, acceptance of gifted peers, and trust in God's goodness.

THE STUNNING GENEROSITY OF THE CROSS

Second, if we hope to lead with humility we must *live in the shadow of the cross*. A few years ago, I had the privilege of speaking at the funeral of our church family's oldest member, Roy. The Lord took him home at 98 years of age. Though the latter years ordinarily tend to sap the energy of most, Roy's twilight years were anything but ordinary. Tennis three times a week, an active life with friends, and a passion for others to know the gospel were the staple of his life right up until his home-going. He was a remarkable man who was admired by all who knew him. I was his pastor only a few short years. In spite of our relatively brief acquaintance, my pursuit of Christ was deeply challenged and refreshed every time we talked. You see, it didn't matter what text I preached on a given Sunday, Roy became visibly overcome with emotion as he contemplated the wonder of the cross. Every redemptive theme, small and great, fell fresh on his heart with each new insight from Scripture. The sweetness of Christ turned ever-sweeter each time he thought of his sin crushing the life of his innocent Lord. As he drew near to the cross I was pulled in and compelled to gaze upon it as he did. Roy had learned that everything we need to know about the Christian life we learn at the foot of Calvary. The cross speaks of the blackness of sin, the holiness of God, and the grace of redeeming love. If we understand the basis for sin's exceeding offensiveness, we will always have a reference point for understanding our unworthiness. C. J. Mahaney, in his book *The Cross-Centered Life*, writes,

> Maybe this thought is nagging you: "If we as Christians have already come to believe in the gospel—if we've already received the gift of salvation He purchased for us with His precious blood—why focus any longer on the cross? Isn't it time to give our full attention to more mature matters of living out the faith?" Nope ... If you think for a moment that the truth of the cross is something you've

already adequately understood ... then ... [already you] have fumbled the most important truth of the Bible, and therefore [will] suffer the consequences.[6]

The theology of the cross must permeate our every affection. Calvary must be our closest and most trusted friend. It's no wonder that Pastor Mahaney once prayed, "Father, I want to stand as close to the cross as I possibly can, because it's harder for me to be arrogant when I'm there."[7] The slow disappearance of the centrality of the cross in our daily lives is subtle. We would never outright deny the significance of Christ's Passion, but its preeminence in our hearts is continually threatened by comparatively insignificant pursuits. If we're unable to recognize the subtleties of lesser affections pleading for our time, we are on a slippery slope into deception. As D. A. Carson warned, "Whenever the periphery is in danger of displacing the center, we are not far removed from idolatry."[8] We cannot allow the wonder and majesty of the cross to grow dim in our understanding. Our thinking must be transformed by seeing the cross from God's frame of reference.

Follow this thought: God cannot abide sin in any degree (Lev 11:44). He is altogether so blazingly pure and righteous that we have no moral ability to comprehend it. What we do know is that when men encountered even a whisper of God's unapproachable light, all kinds of bizarre experiences ensued. Moses' countenance glowed (Exod 34:29–30), Isaiah considered himself instantly and utterly ruined (Isa 6:5), Peter, James, and John fell to the ground terrified (Matt 17:6), and the pen-prolific Paul, after visiting heaven, wasn't allowed to offer a single intelligible word to

---

6   C. J. Mahaney, *Living The Cross-Centered Life* (Colorado Springs, CO: Multnomah Books, 2006), 17.

7   C. J. Mahaney, *Humility*, 68.

8   D. A. Carson, *The Cross and Christian Ministry: Leadership Lessons from 1 Corinthians* (Grand Rapids, MI: Baker Books, 2004), 26.

describe the experience (2 Cor 12:4)! What's my point? When we see God's holiness we begin to grasp the magnitude of His love displayed toward condemned sinners. First John 4:9 says, "In this the love of God was made manifest among us, that God sent his only Son into the world, so that we might live through him." At the cross we are confronted with a kind of love that invites mercy into the courtroom of holy justice, and the Judge offers His own life as the peace offering. Instead of facing eternal hell, we were reconciled to a holy God while judgment fell on Christ.

And if that weren't profound enough, it is beyond comprehension that such reconciliation would come as wrath was poured out upon a holy, pure, innocent, and righteous subject! Make no mistake, the undefiled Son of God was as immeasurably delightful to His Father as sinners are repulsive, yet He was afflicted for our redemption. Oh, how such a love should humble our proud hearts. When we become bitter at "injustices" against us, the cross reminds us that every earthly injustice, no matter how offensive to our sensibilities, could never parallel the holy offense caused by a sinner's guilt placed upon the innocent Lamb of God. We sent Christ to the cross. It was our sin that crushed His pure heart, our guilt He undeservedly embraced. When we begin to live in light of the real offense of the cross, humility will constrain our thoughts and attitudes. We will begin to lead with love and compassion. How can I—a sinner saved by grace—take advantage of God's people, elevating myself above fellow-recipients of God's love? What right do I have to be harsh with those I lead, or to withhold loving kindness when my ministry isn't appreciated? I'm simply a steward of the riches of God's grace, having been entrusted with the privilege and responsibility of delivering gospel truth. All truly humble leadership must begin here. D. A. Carson takes this thought further, calling the Western church to repentance:

> In the West, we must repent of our endless fascination
> for "leadership" that smacks much more either of hier-
> archical models (I am the boss, and, for all below me

on the ladder, what I say goes) or of democratic models (give the people what they want; take another survey, conduct another poll, and scratch where they itch). All valid Christian leadership, however varied its style, however wise its use of sociological findings, however diverse its functions, must begin with this fundamental recognition: Christian leaders have been entrusted with the gospel, the secret things of God that have been hidden in ages past but that are now proclaimed, by their ministry, to men and women everywhere.[9]

Our problems are exacerbated when we forget how quickly our hearts move away from the truth. We have a dreadful tendency to overestimate our ability to stay on course. "Drifting" into self-sufficiency and apathy happens when we presume to know what we can and cannot handle. This reality sank deep into my heart recently while reading a collection of letters written by C. John Miller[10] to pastors and ministry leaders all over the world. While encouraging a fellow missionary serving in Ireland, the characteristically transparent "Jack" Miller wrote the following:

> Perhaps you don't drift the way that I do, but I constantly forget the deep hole of depravity from which the Lord's mighty love rescued me. Drifting does not take any effort at all; just stop cultivating the knowledge of Christ, and the evil current of secularism does the rest. All passion for the lost seems increasingly a fading memory. Jesus weeping over Jerusalem, Paul willing to be cursed for

---

9   Ibid., 96.

10   C. John Miller ("Jack") taught practical theology at Westminster Theological Seminary, was director of World Harvest Mission, and was the founding pastor of New Life Presbyterian Church, Philadelphia, PA. His correspondence was compiled and edited by his daughter, Barbara Miller Juliani.

the sake of his countrymen, those things become very remote to the point of being unreal.[11]

Dependence upon God is our only way of escaping such arrogant folly. We do well to recall the apostle Peter's rapid descent into failure, recorded in Matthew 26:31–35. One dramatic evening, the Master Himself gave the disciples the scorecard of the human heart: "You will all fall away because of me this night" (v. 31). They should have been on their faces, pleading with the Lord for strengthening grace! Sadly, Peter spoke for all followers of Christ that day when he opened his mouth presumptuously: "Though they all fall away because of you, I will never fall away" (v. 33). This particular disease infects us at so many levels. Instead of being ever-dependent on divine truth, we assume that our privileged relationship with Christ is somehow a result of our own goodness.

The sin of presumption comes from believing that being a child of God *makes us* personally significant. Or worse, and far more sinister, we may begin to think we belong to God *because* we are significant. When we believe we know our hearts better than the God who made us, it is presumption. When we argue with the Word of God, questioning its perfect wisdom for our lives, it is audacity! Humility doesn't question the goodness of God's purposes. Peter's plunge into spiritual weakness began when his foolish heart rose up to rebuke the Lord for speaking of impending torture and death (Matt 16:22). Jesus' reply would be etched into Peter's heart for the rest of his life as a reminder never to lean on his own understanding: "Get behind me, Satan! You are a hindrance to me. For you are not setting your mind on the things of God, but on the things of man" (v. 23). Our fleshly ambitions are duly starved when we yield to the plans and purposes of God,

---

11   C. John Miller, *The Heart of a Servant Leader*, ed. Barbara Miller Juliani (Phillipsburg, NJ: P&R Publishing, 2004), 70.

especially when our questions go unanswered. The cross of Christ teaches us to rest in the knowledge that if God was willing to reconcile us while we were enemies, then we can trust Him to lead us in the way of abundant life. Humility is the fruit of willingly coming under His perfect leadership.

Admittedly, it's easier to talk of being humbly obedient than to cultivate the discipline required to grow its lasting roots. It's a bit like the husband and wife who were contemplating a trip to the Holy Land:

> *Husband*: "Wouldn't it be fantastic to go to the Holy Land and stand and shout the Ten Commandments from Mount Sinai?"

> *Wife*: "It would be better if we stayed home and kept them."[12]

Until God's unshakeable Word saturates our minds and shatters our wills, we cannot hope to make Christ our highest affection. Our superlative model is the Lord Jesus Christ. The Father's will was His supreme pleasure. He was anchored to divine promises and therefore "continued entrusting himself to him who judges justly" (1 Pet 2:23). In Philippians 2:5–8 Paul appeals to the example of Christ's stunning generosity, challenging us to cultivate this same quality of obedience. The apostle knows that a healthy doctrine of salvation is the only thing that will crush our pride and mold us into humble shepherds of God's people. If our leadership would exude humility, it will reflect the same lavish sacrifice shown by our Lord in His incarnation. Before coming to earth, the second member of the Trinity existed eternally, the God of the universe, robed in splendor, and finding undiminished

---

12   "Can You See the Signs?" (2006–2009) at http://powerpointsermons.com/?page=study&type= ir&sermon_id=74&res_num=&print=1&select_id=15583.

pleasure in Himself (Phil 2:6a). And though the glory of sovereign rule was rightfully His to enjoy, He didn't seize it as a coveted possession when sinners were in desperate need of being rescued (Phil 2:6b). If Christ was so generous to His enemies, we must never grab and clutch at position, power, or status. In self-humiliation, our Lord descended from splendor to slave, willingly shrouding His heavenly glory in a life of submissive dependence (Phil 2:7). Paul uses the New Testament word *doulos* to convey the concept of slavery. The Son of God became the slave of God!

Is this how we lead? Do we readily yield our will as "bondslaves" of the plans and purposes of Christ? He came in the likeness of sinners to purchase their redemption. Surely, I can lay aside personal comforts and earthly securities to see God's people abundantly reach the glories of heaven. Our Lord performed no miracles in order to make His life more convenient; He made no secret use of supernatural power for personal gain. His bold self-testimony was that "the Son can do nothing of his own accord, but only what He sees the Father doing. For whatever the Father does, that the Son does likewise" (John 5:19). The flint of His heart ignited only the flame of His Father's will, and when the temptation to grab earthly greatness hammered Him from every side, He humbly forfeited the safety of human approval, saying, "Not what I will, but what you will" (Mark 14:36). Indeed, He entered an evil world as a helpless, vulnerable infant without the pageantry befitting the King of Kings. Few men have articulated it better than John Eadie:

> From His possession of this "mind," [Phil 2:5] and in indescribable generosity He looked at the things of others, and descended with His splendour eclipsed—appeared not as a God in glory, but clothed in flesh; not in royal robes, but in the dress of a village youth; not as Deity in fire, but a man in tears; not in a palace, but in a manger;

not with a thunderbolt in His hand, but with the hatchet
and hammer of a Galilean mechanic.[13]

If we aspire to lead with humility, we must be willing to die
to all that we hold dear. At the cross, we have been "crucified
with Christ" (Gal 2:20) in order that "those who live might no
longer live for themselves but for him who for their sake died and
was raised" (2 Cor 5:15). Godly leadership is an exchange of our
reputation for the glory of His, our expectations for the joy of His
yoke, and our personal gain for His perfect design.

A WRETCH LIKE ME

Finally, leading with humility requires a *well-traveled understanding of human depravity.* One of the greatest dangers of spiritual
leadership is to continue giving counsel and instruction to others
without serious examination of one's own soul. A thoroughly biblical grasp of our fallen condition compels us to "preach to ourselves" before we attempt to lead others. There are few things
more challenging than dealing with a leader who condescends to
others as though he needed only small doses of grace by comparison. Such men regularly minimize their own failings by speaking
at those under their care. If the pattern continues unchecked,
their love for the saints becomes aloof cordiality, biblical counsel loses all necessary tenderness, and expressions of humility are
merely for show.

The Gospel of Luke records a parable Jesus told featuring an
outcast who knew the blackness of his own heart and a Pharisee
whose self-righteousness blinded him to the spiritual bankruptcy
within. It's the classic story of the "haves" and the "have nots."
Here's the account:

---

13   John Eadie, *A Commentary on the Greek Text of the Epistle of Paul to the Philippians* (Eugene,
OR: Wipf and Stock Publishers, 1998), 107.

He also told this parable to some who trusted in them-selves that they were righteous, and treated others with contempt: "Two men went up into the temple to pray, one a Pharisee and the other a tax collector. The Pharisee, standing by himself, prayed thus: 'God, I thank you that I am not like other men, extortioners, unjust, adulterers, or even like this tax collector. I fast twice a week; I give tithes of all that I get.' But the tax collector, standing far off, would not even lift up his eyes to heaven, but beat his breast, saying, 'God, be merciful to me, a sinner!' I tell you, this man went down to his house justified, rather than the other. For everyone who exalts himself will be humbled, but the one who humbles himself will be exalted." (Luke 18:9–14)

The tax collector—a traitor to his country—saw his sin con-dition in all its wicked hue, while the doctor of theology felt quite content that he was "acceptable" before God. Jesus' point is unmistakable: Those who see their depravity rightly preach to themselves before they presume to examine another. A proud heart seeks to run from culpability, setting up a sophisticated labyrinth of excuses for why the good should outweigh all other "relatively minor" infractions. The tax collector, however, in bro-kenness, saw the avarice that made him a traitor. He was wicked through and through, and he knew it. He met the enemy that day, and the enemy was himself! And though the parable's point is how pride prevents true conversion, its implications regarding humility in general are piercing. The moment we imagine we've exhaus-tively assessed the sin of our hearts, we have planted, watered, and harvested a crop of pride. Using the prophet Jeremiah as His mouthpiece, God said, "The heart is deceitful above all things, and desperately sick; who can understand it? I, the LORD, search the heart and test the mind" (Jer 17:9–10). What tills the soil of humble leadership is the knowledge of our dreadful love of rebel-lion. Taking full ownership of our moral poverty turns our spiritual influence into a work of grace, preventing laziness and pride. It causes us to ask penetrating questions about our character and work hard at true change. The result is a compassion for others who struggle to gain ground in their sanctification because we are intimately acquainted with our own weakness.

Seeing our sin rightly will also prevent a growing cynicism and lack of love for the lost. As Thomas Murphy carefully notes,

> It is important for [the preacher's] own sake, it is important for his people's sake, that he should preach every sermon to himself as one of the chief auditors ... even when he is addressing the [unbeliever], for their hearts and his are by nature alike, and the gulf from which he would draw them is the gulf from which he has only narrowly escaped himself.[14]

The people of God thrive under a humble leader. Meekness is best cultivated when we are confronted with the majesty and glory of Almighty God. When His significance, not ours, is the captivating principle of our affections, we will lead with humility. As the profound offense and incomprehensible love of the cross permeate our thinking, we will say with John the Baptist, "He must increase, but I must decrease" (John 3:30). If we will never let a day slip by without being reminded of our propensity to drift into sluggish self-sufficiency, then those who follow our example will find it a blessed path.

> O Lord, keeping a humble heart is so difficult. Everything in me resists it. I see Your majesty in creation and on the pages of Scripture, but far too often I steal Your glory in prideful self-seeking. I need Your grace to see the cross rightly; I want to know the

---

14   Thomas Murphy, *Pastoral Theology* (Audubon, NJ: Old Paths Publications, 1996), 81.

horror of the cross that I may never forget the treachery of my sin and the stunning generosity of grace; I long to be consumed with the loveliness of Christ so that I always make much of You! Give me discernment to recognize when I stray from these wonders. Amen.

THE FREEDOM OF
INTEGRITY

I once heard a story about a traveling salesman who was delivering a compelling presentation to the executive manager of a large company. As he was about to unveil the "bottom line" cost of his offer, the executive excused himself for a brief moment. In his absence, the salesman's eyes caught his rival company's letterhead on the desk. Noticing that it was a proposal, he strained to see his opponent's cost figures at the bottom of the page, which were unfortunately covered by the executive's soda can. Unable to restrain his curiosity and seeking to gain an advantage, he quickly lifted the can, which suddenly unleashed hundreds of tiny steel pellets, sending them all over the desk and office floor. The shocked salesman hung his head, promptly packed up his proposal, and slipped away in shame. His integrity had been tested, and he failed. The anecdotal tale graphically illustrates the importance of cultivating a heart of honesty and sincerity—a reputation for saying and living the same thing.

To boil it down, integrity is the consistent harmony of convictions and conduct. Leaders who unswervingly live according to the principles they claim as inviolable are full of integrity. The opposite, of course, is hypocrisy. For *spiritual* leaders, the Word of God is our incontestable standard! Our convictions must come from Scripture and our conduct brought into conformity with its directives. Where there is doctrinal compromise there has long been a contentedness "with unbiblical notions that raise [the] comfort level and either justify or overlook ... sins."[1] Integrity is having an untarnished moral character both publicly and *when no one else is around.*

Leaders can become adept at disguising reproachable conduct, hiding behind moral sleight-of-hand techniques, intimidation, or important titles. Eventually, dishonest men convince even themselves of their "invincibility" until their hypocrisy is exposed in some scandal. When a spiritual leader's mask comes off and God's people are forced to deal with the fallout, the frequent result is an acknowledgement that certain "signs" of diminishing integrity were overlooked. During the months following a character crisis at the leadership level, there has been a common tendency to imagine that an otherwise decent leader simply stumbled one day into moral weakness, caught off guard by an overpowering temptation. Such conclusions are naïve. A ministry mentor, John MacArthur, has said to me on numerous occasions that "when a man falls, he doesn't fall far." In other words, a serious breach of leadership integrity does not occur in a vacuum. Men who have, by the grace of God, forged a pattern of moral veracity are not suddenly seduced by a life of lies and hypocrisy. Betrayal of this sort slowly percolates in the heart over time with a host of smaller, virtually undetected compromises. When an integrity scandal breaks, the fall of that leader is more like a short hop! This is not to suggest that godliness makes us immune to Satan's schemes or our own fleshly appetites. MacArthur is right, however, to imply that where genuine biblical integrity has been refined, there is the strong traction of spiritual discernment and fortitude which prevents sudden moral plunges. Before enticing interests gain a foothold, men of settled integrity have already unmasked the lie

---

1   John MacArthur, *The Power of Integrity* (Wheaton, IL: Crossway Books, 1997), 30.

and fled the scene as fast as possible (1 Tim 6:11; 2 Tim 2:22; Heb 5:14). On this topic, Spurgeon's eloquence is unmatched: "When we hear of a man who has ruined his character by a surprising act of folly, we may surmise, as a rule, that this mischief was but one sulphurous jet from a soil charged with volcanic fire; or, to change the figure, one roaring lion from a den of wild beasts.[2]

INTEGRITY AND THE CONSCIENCE

A heart of integrity is cultivated by *striving to maintain a clear conscience*. Our conscience is the internal mechanism given to us by God to drive us toward sincerity. Like an internal accountability partner, it acts as a witness in our heart and mind to either "accuse or even excuse" our actions (Rom 2:15). When we inform the conscience with biblical truth we are telling it to accurately hold us in check against the standard of Scripture. The conscience itself is not our benchmark, but if kept clear and clean it becomes a powerful instrument of integrity as it drives us toward the grand, inflexible benchmark—God's Word.

There is grave danger when a leader ignores the cries of the conscience. All discernment is lost, pride blooms aggressively, and self-deception spins out of control. The young pastor, Timothy, was warned by the apostle Paul to keep "a good conscience" (1 Tim 1:19), citing Hymenaeus and Alexander as two contemporaries who regularly violated the convictions they smugly affirmed (1 Tim 1:20). Paul knew that an insincere faith and marred conscience would lead to "vain discussion," sinful ambition, and the propagation of heresy (1 Tim 1:6–7). He spoke often about the spiritual devastation resulting from the conscience being repeatedly snubbed:

---

2   C. H. Spurgeon, *An All-Round Ministry* (1900; repr., Edinburgh, Banner of Truth, 2000), 137.

- "For if anyone sees you who have knowledge eating in an idol's temple, will he not be encouraged, if his conscience is weak, to eat food offered to idols? And so by your knowledge this weak person is destroyed, the brother for whom Christ died. Thus, sinning against your brothers and *wounding* their conscience when it is weak, you sin against Christ" (1 Cor 8:10–12).

- "This charge I entrust to you … wage the good warfare, holding faith and a good conscience. By rejecting this, some have made *shipwreck* of their faith" (1 Tim 1:18–19).

- "Now the Spirit expressly says that in later times some will depart from the faith … through the insincerity of liars whose consciences are *seared*" (1 Tim 4:1–2).

- "To the pure, all things are pure, but to the defiled and unbelieving, nothing is pure; but both their minds and their consciences are *defiled*" (Titus 1:15).

Paul's language is unmistakably that of spiritual detriment. Each time our conscience "sounds off" we can either muffle or unleash the volume of its impact. Prompt obedience sharpens the clarity of truth's familiar sound, causing our spiritual senses to go on high alert. The more we obey, the greater affirmation that we are honest and genuine. A highly trained, truth-sensitive conscience will give us no rest when we edge toward compromise. If, instead of resolutely fleeing sin, we suppress the truth in rationalization and compromise, the clearest resonation of right and wrong will become faint. Do this enough times and no bell of truth will ring at all! What appears to others as a life of faithfulness will merely be the calm before the storm. Time and truth always go hand in hand, and the small, seemingly insignificant compromises of today will erode tomorrow's resolve. How can we build and maintain a life of integrity so that our leadership is worthy of being modeled?

A TRUTH-SENSITIVE INNER LIFE

Besides watching people reject Christ, the most devastating experience of a spiritual leader is to have his genuine, heartfelt, compassionate, honest, and truthful service spoken of as evil. To have your hard-forged integrity maligned is, in a word, agony! It's difficult enough being misunderstood, but deliberate misrepresentation is like a dagger thrust into your passion for shepherding. What's so astonishing about a leader like the apostle Paul are his many bold claims about having a completely clean conscience. At his defense before the Jewish Council, he asserted, "I have lived my life before God in all good conscience up to this day" (Acts 23:1). A short time later, at a public hearing in Caesarea, Paul told the governor, "I always take pains to have a clear conscience toward both God and man" (Acts 24:16). He frequently appealed to the internal witness of God as the ultimate answer to questions of honesty (2 Cor 1:12; 4:2; 1 Thess 2:4; 2 Tim 1:3). It seems clear that, for Paul, maintaining a life of integrity involved the strict discipline of protecting a truth-sensitive conscience at all costs. Hard work and personal vigilance were a given if his ministry was to experience maximum blessing. In fact, he once told the Corinthian church that he strikes out against the appetites of his flesh to bring his life into slavery lest he be disqualified from leadership (1 Cor 9:27). His primary motivation for learning self-control was to obtain the "imperishable" trophy of gospel fruit (1 Cor 9:23–26).

But what were Paul's non-negotiables for cultivating and preserving leadership integrity? We get a glimpse of his heart from a study of 1 Thessalonians, where the integrity of leadership is explained and defended with an appeal to the exemplary ministry of his traveling missionary team. After approximately three months of explosive ministry in Thessalonica, some of the Jews had begun a sophisticated smear campaign against the character of Paul and his friends, claiming that they had served for personal power, prestige, and money (1 Thess 2:3–12), that they had abandoned this new church in its hour of need (2:17–20), and that they had deceived the new converts by concealing the trouble such new beliefs would bring (3:2–4). Paul was no stranger to scurrilous charges, but defending his personal honor was never his agenda. On the contrary, he always met accusations by appealing to the life-on-life interaction of his ministry. Repeated phrases in chapter 2 such as "You yourselves know," "As you know," "For you recall," and "You are witnesses" exemplify Paul's transparency in everything he said and did.

AN OPEN BOOK

The first of Paul's principles of integrity, therefore, is to *invite open scrutiny*. Integrity is cultivated "out in the open" where others can observe whether your words match your actions. Paul was willing to appeal to the specific history and details of his ministry, offering them up to a full examination of the facts. He had no worry that the Thessalonians would find even the slightest lack of genuine care, personal sacrifice, and humble service. If they would carefully weigh each slanderous charge against the evidence from his leadership, they would be compelled to see the situation rightly. "But surely Paul failed at times, didn't he?" someone may counter. He is human after all, and we would expect him to miscue on occasion—speak a harsh word, act selfishly, or take credit for achievements. But Paul was so consistently characterized by humility about his apostleship that if someone discovered a flaw, they found his brokenness and contrition as irresistible as his strengths. Consequently, he was free to invite open scrutiny because his ministry, theology, and effectiveness were not a sham or "personally derived." Likewise, our theology and character should not be about our success or achievements, but about finding the clarity of the truth and living it. When someone disagrees or misrepresents our life and ministry, we shouldn't be personally threatened by the resulting scrutiny. Paul was truly free of all such concern, and so he boldly asked that the Thessalonians check the slanderous claims against their experience with him as a leader in their midst!

NOT AS PLEASING MEN

His second non-negotiable of integrity is to *serve with spiritual courage*. The Thessalonians were being told that the missionaries were hirelings, speaking bold words to gain power over them, but who would abandon the sheep at the first sign of opposition. Jesus had chided hirelings who feign protection but are cowards in the face of danger (John 10:11–15). Self-preservation at all costs is a weakness, not a virtue. But was it true of Paul and the others? Again, he appeals to the spiritual courage they had demonstrated some one hundred miles to the northeast in the city of Philippi. Even after they had "suffered and been shamefully treated," they "had boldness in ... God to declare ... the gospel of God in the midst of much conflict" (1 Thess 2:2). Paul literally hobbled into Thessalonica—blood still drying on his body from the beating in Philippi—and began to teach in the synagogue, the most confrontational and dangerous environment the truth of Christ could infiltrate. After several weeks (perhaps two to three months) of unvarnished gospel ministry, the truth hit hard upon stony hearts, at which point the missionaries were secretly whisked away by the new believers who wanted to preserve the lives of their only trusted shepherds. I can almost hear Paul, reluctant to be sent away, strongly contending for the opportunity to remain and teach yet again in the synagogue.

Are these the actions of a man without integrity? The answer is a resounding "No!" A godly man has nothing to fear because his conscience has been "approved by God to be entrusted with the gospel," and he speaks "not as pleasing men, but to please God" who sees what is in the heart (1 Thess 2:4). Solomon, not to be outdone, declared that "The wicked flee when no one pursues, but the righteous are bold as a lion" (Prov 28:1). Check spiritual leaders! Do they demonstrate spiritual courage? Do they trust the work and the Word of God? Do they unfold the Scriptures without shrinking back? Do they give an answer with biblical clarity? Do they willingly invite questions about doctrine, ministry, character, service, etc.? If not, the sheep will become vulnerable, and slander will eventually have its way in the church. Integrity marked by courageous leadership is a tremendous safeguard.

BATTLES ONLY GOD CAN SEE

A third non-negotiable of integrity is an *unashamed transparency before God*. A leader must consistently win the battles of his own heart if he is to lead with sincere and genuine effectiveness. Obviously, Paul knew that his heart wasn't blameless in the war against his flesh. Though subject to failure like any sinner, he wasn't in the habit of rationalizing or excusing infractions of God's holy standard, and therefore freely summoned the incisive witness of his Creator. In 1 Thessalonians 2:4–5 Paul states, "Just as we have been approved by God to be entrusted with the gospel, so we speak, not to please man, but to please God who tests our hearts. For we never came with words of flattery, as you know, nor with a pretext for greed—God is witness." As to questions of doctrinal error, prurient interests, flattering speech, or greed, Paul and the missionaries proved to be earnest and truthful. If the case were otherwise, how could Paul speak strongly in the face of opposition without fear of contradiction? Were his heart set on using the Thessalonians for personal gain, he could have no such confidence, no such liberal invoking of divine examination.

Those who neglect the issues of the heart must develop elaborate ways of working around the truth. Like a master chess player, a leader who rationalizes sin carefully calculates every evasive move and counter-argument. He may appear composed to his followers, but deep within there is a cauldron of desires being cleverly excused in a deadly game of cat and mouse. Rationalization is the well-worn tool of the dishonest and insincere. Its familiar progression is easily sketched:

- Temptation arises and the conscience warns of impending danger. *Rationalization*: "Because I already hate sin as a general rule, I can be near temptation without desiring it or becoming vulnerable."

- Temptation intensifies. *Rationalization*: "I've been doing well spiritually, what possible damage could result from merely 'noticing' trouble?"

- Sinful desires begin to consume the thought life. *Rationalization*: "My life is very difficult, so how am I supposed to be strong all the time? Can I be expected to hold off every powerful enticement when I'm under such pressure?"

- The conscience screams reminders about truth, family, friends, and consequences. *Rationalization*: "Since I'm alone, none of those I love will be affected; and besides, this is a small sin compared to what I've seen others do."

- Sin prevails with the attendant guilt. *Rationalization*: "I'm not as bad as others; I know God will forgive me; I'll just leave this between me and Him; I don't need anyone's help because they'll just be judgmental."

- Sin continues as a pattern, truth becomes dull, and sensations of guilt fade. *Rationalization*: "People can be so legalistic; they think they're the only ones who do anything right. God is much more loving and He wants me to be happy."

While the above doesn't capture all the tactics of the heart, it does depict the general anatomy of compromise. In the concise words of Proverbs 18:1, "Whoever isolates himself seeks his own desire; he breaks out against all sound judgment." No matter what outward successes or popularity contests grace a leader's trophy case, rationalization always gives birth to sin and ruin (Jas 1:14–15). Halting this terrible process requires the radical amputation of sinful desires, the complete ownership of failure through confession and repentance, and mind renewal by the saturation of Scripture and submission of the will. The prevention of sin, Jesus said, begins with *radical surgery* at the level of our affections:

> You have heard that it was said, "You shall not commit adultery." But I say to you that everyone who looks at a woman with lustful intent has already committed adultery with her in his heart. If your right eye causes you to sin, tear it out and throw it away. For it is better that you lose one of your members than that your whole body be thrown into hell. And if your right hand causes you to sin, cut it off and throw it away. For it is better that you lose one of your members than that your whole body go into hell. (Matt 5:27–30)

The moment our minds entertain a sinful desire we must "flee these things" (1 Tim 6:11), running as fast as we can to take refuge in the cross of our Lord and Master. Furthermore, rationalization cannot coexist with a full disclosure and *ownership of sin*. David's confession in Psalm 51 is filled with expressions of personal responsibility:

> According to your abundant mercy, blot out my transgressions. Wash me thoroughly from my iniquity and cleanse me from my sin! For I know my transgressions, and my sin is ever before me. Against you, you only, have I sinned and done what is evil in your sight, so that you may be justified in your words and blameless in your judgment (vv. 1–4).

True confession involves seeing sin as God defines it, without mitigation or blurring the lines. Taking ownership of every nuance of offense caused by our sin and bearing the weight of it—this is the heart of the truly penitent. The premier evidence that we have genuinely "owned" our sin is the desire to exonerate God's character in the matter. Rather than justifying himself, David extolled the justice of God in every consequence resulting from sin ("blameless in your judgment," v. 4). Lest we think otherwise, such personal responsibility was no picnic for the king of Israel! Shortly after the writing of Psalm 51, rationalizing his sin plunged David into nearly thirty years of devastating family turmoil and years of insipid leadership surrounding him. Through it all, he never accused God of being overly harsh or unfair. David's heart was broken and sincere, the kind of repentance with which God is highly pleased (Ps 51:17). When a leader is "a man after [God's] own heart" (1 Sam 13:14), rationalization finds no place.

LIVING BY EVERY WORD

Finally, it is much harder to rationalize sin when *our minds are saturated with the Word of God and our wills are swiftly brought into subjection.* We need clear definitions of sin, lofty views of God's majestic holiness, and the perfect guidance of the Holy Spirit to fashion in us the character of Christ. If we desire divine power against temptation but neglect the "milk of the Word," the Spirit has nothing to work with since it is His truth alone that He uses to sanctify (John 17:17). As MacArthur simply states, "Divine truth and godliness are inextricably related. No matter how sincere our intentions might be, we cannot obey God's will if we do not know what it is. We cannot be godly if we do not know what God is like and what He expects of those who belong to Him."[3]

---

3   MacArthur, *Integrity*, 38.

On the other hand, if we study Scripture without yielding our will, then our lives will change very little, and the risk of becoming a Pharisee will increase. Ezra "set his heart to study the Law of the LORD, and *to do it* ... " (Ezra 7:10) because he knew there was no profit for his mind and heart otherwise. Spiritual leaders cement their integrity by learning early the value of yielding to "every word that comes from the mouth of God" (Matt 4:4). If our motives for study and meditation are spurious, driven largely by curiosity, obligation, or intellectual pride, there will be "no real benefit to the soul."[4]

Integrity is an anchor for effective spiritual leadership and influence. When truth is at home in our hearts, God smiles upon meager efforts, covering our limitations with His grace and wisdom. As the people of Israel used to sing, "O LORD, who may ... dwell on Your holy hill? He who walks with integrity, and works righteousness, and speaks truth in his heart" (Ps 15:1–2, NASB).

> *Dear Savior, help me to do battle where no one else can see but You. If my conscience cries out, may I never suppress it in a foolish rationalization. Make me see the subtle gymnastics of my heart, and compel me to take full ownership of my sin. May Your grace lead me to true repentance so that I remain highly sensitive to the truth. Amen.*

---

4   A. W. Pink, *Profiting from the Word* (Carlisle, PA: Banner of Truth Trust, 1970), 10.

5

STAMINA FOR
THE LONG HAUL

Some time ago, I asked a very prominent pastor of many battle-worn years what he saw as the most needed quality among church leaders today. Without a moment's hesitation, he emphatically replied, "Faithfulness!" Above all other worthy qualities, steadfast endurance immediately topped this seasoned shepherd's list. Even though he places a high premium on essential traits like humility, sacrifice, integrity, discipline, and wisdom, none of these immediately overshadowed the desperate call for faithfulness. But it occurred to me that a man of so many years would have witnessed the frequent defection of leaders from their sacred privilege and responsibility. He was all too familiar with those who begin the marathon of leadership in a burst of promising speed and giftedness, only to be disqualified by neglect, pretense, or abdication. Many men start their ministry with a servant's heart, but disillusionment can set in after years of serving alongside those who never reciprocate. In spite of a strong commitment to integrity, others experience personal failure and ministry disappointment which tempt them to hide in hypocrisy. Even the ability to inspire and mobilize others to reach goals, if selfishly motivated, can lead to distrust and hopelessness. It's simply hard to remain steadfast through all the complexities and problems that come with the territory. In fact, without the power of the Holy Spirit, it is impossible!

It is the cultivation of godly character, practiced *over the long haul* that has lasting and profound effectiveness. The legacy of other faithful Christian leaders throughout church history calls us to carefully consider our stewardship, leaving no room for excuses. Increasingly, ours is a generation of shallow convictions, malnourished skills, and low moral fiber among leaders. Books continue to be written and leadership resources offered at break-neck speed. With all that is available one would expect that, as with a time-tested automobile, the basic frame and power plant of ministry would be well oiled. By now, the church should be adept at identifying, cultivating, and replicating strong Christian leaders who demonstrate a long-term faithfulness in the same direction.[1] Where are such individuals? The new generation of ministry architects is all about cultural fads, trendy innovations, and anti-establishment ideologies. It's no wonder that when God's people need leaders who can navigate the treacherous waters of spiritual warfare, they find no one at the helm to provide biblical clarity and model battle stamina.

STRENGTHENED BY GRACE

Many times in the struggle of ministry I've needed encouragement to press on. And God is so meticulous in His care of us that He places in our path friends who offer the right word at just the right moment—a timely "pep-talk," if you will, that energizes our hearts for one more thrust of the sword! While deadlocked in a struggle to remain steadfast, Paul's young apprentice, Timothy, was in need of one of those "come-to-Jesus" talks from his father in the faith. With the balance of a seasoned shepherd, Paul gave

---

1   Adapted from *A Long Obedience in the Same Direction*, Eugene H. Petersen, (Downers Grove, IL: Intervarsity Christian Fellowship, 1980).

Timothy this admonition: "You then, my child, be strengthened by the grace that is in Christ Jesus. … Share in suffering as a good soldier of Christ Jesus. No soldier gets entangled in civilian pursuits, since his aim is to please the one who enlisted him" (2 Tim 2:1, 3–4). What a tremendous call to battle! Essentially, an older, more seasoned soldier reminds his inexperienced friend that everything in ministry is completely dependent upon the purposes, battle plan, and reinforcements from headquarters. The grace that *saves* the sinner is the power that must *supply* the sinner.

Someone may ask, "How can Paul urge Timothy to be strong if it is God's grace that strengthens?" We must remember that the Christian life is a walk of faith—entrusting ourselves to the promises of God in all things (2 Cor 5:7). Timothy is being called upon to use, with commitment and confidence, the divine provisions he had already been given through the grace of Christ. In the heat of battle, faithful leaders do not require a divine reversal of circumstances or immediate answers to every challenge. They take a stand, "work[ing] out [their] own salvation with fear and trembling" (Phil 2:12), knowing that as they yield their will to God, He infuses their labors with supernatural power. Sometimes we go to God for spiritual strength, expecting Him to dispense some blast of supernatural "juice" that catapults us past our present difficulty. The key to solving this paradox is the *submission of the will*. What kind of faith would it be if every time we faced a temptation, God moved in and "pushed us into obedience"? Faithfulness is not forged in passivity. God's power will sustain us, but the *means* by which divine strength is enjoyed is our proactive striving (Phil 2:12-13).

The focal point of our labor is the "grace that is in Christ Jesus." Show me someone who seems to always rise above the din of life's hardships, and I'll show you someone who ponders redemption deeply, and presses on in faith! The grace in which we stand (Rom 5:2), by which we battle sin (Rom 6:4–11), and through which we are kept until glory (Jude 20–21), causes us to persevere against all odds.

GET IN THE FLOW

"And what you have heard from me in the presence of many witnesses entrust to faithful men who will be able to teach others also" (2 Tim 2:2). Timothy is further urged to pass the ministry baton to steadfast men who, having discharged their responsibility as servant-leaders, are to cultivate another crop of godly men, entrusting to them the mandate of leadership endurance.

One of the great thrills of my life is the frequent privilege of deep theological discussions with my father. When he reached seventy years of age he began taking classes in biblical Hebrew and systematic theology. He is a voracious reader and constantly peppers me with questions about what he should be reading next. My earliest memories of his conversion are of his early morning Bible reading and endless hours of discipleship with other men from the church. He was thirty-three when the Lord's grace pierced his heart and began to radically transform our home life. You might assume that with the passing of time and years of spiritual warfare, my dad's passion for truth and burden for the church would lose steam. Quite the opposite! In fact, with my mother ever-faithful at his side, their collective spiritual stamina is a tremendous legacy given to our family. All the grandchildren and great grandchildren know that at regular intervals they will be challenged by their "Granddad" to "press on toward the goal for the prize of the upward call of God in Christ Jesus" (Phil 3:14). Years ago, my dad calculated that if his four boys each had four children of their own, and the trend continued for five generations, his life would have a direct impact on more than 250 souls. That sobering equation served to fuel his passion for a gospel-driven life. Whenever I'm tempted to complain under the strain of ministry, I'm suddenly convicted, knowing that my dad has not ceased striving to know his Savior and the power of Christ's resurrection.

Are you ready to leave such a legacy of faithfulness? Getting in the flow of discipleship is a sacred trust that cries out for immoveable convictions, demonstrated in the perpetual replication of fellow leaders. The ministry privileges afforded Timothy were rich indeed. Having learned the gospel from a faithful mother and grandmother (2 Tim 1:5; 3:15), he was in a long line of truth-bearers. He regularly sat under excellent preaching; he was personally mentored by godly influences; he did his pastoral residency under the apostle Paul! For years he had been exposed to the truth, and was now accountable as a steward. Turning back or abandoning his responsibility was not an option. Being "in the flow" means learning as much as possible, identifying others who will safeguard the truth, articulating the truth to them, and maturing them until they can replicate the cycle.

Weakness spreads rapidly when leaders are lazy or isolated from the flow of discipleship and mentoring. One halfhearted link in the chain jeopardizes the strength of the whole enterprise. Committed leaders are not satisfied with mediocrity where the "gray twilight ... knows not victory nor defeat."[2] One of the greatest deterrents to sin in my life comes from knowing that so many have invested time, resources, prayers, and godliness in me. How can I be less than persevering in the shadow of those who have gone before and in the face of so many who now look to me for leadership? And beyond leaving a faithful legacy to those who follow, our resolve should flow from the desire to rightly represent our covenant-keeping God. His unimpeachable love is our high mark—our singular aim. Though never presuming to match His glorious covenant love, we should strenuously labor to bear the marks of His commitment.

Using three vivid analogies in 2 Timothy 2, Paul captures the essence of unflinching devotion in the soldier's desire to obey his commander, the athlete's disciplined path to victory, and the tireless farmer's well-earned reward. Each portrayal highlights the

---

2   Theodore Roosevelt, "The Strenuous Life," Speech before the Hamilton Club, Chicago, Delivered April 10, 1899, http://www.theodore-roosevelt.com/trstrenlife.html (accessed December 6, 2007).

primacy of faithfulness in spite of the hardships and self-sacrifice required to succeed. What motivates a leader to endure the overwhelming odds against him in the battles of ministry? Surely, it isn't the shallow promises of cultural acceptance, a sense of community, organizational teamwork, or being "relevant." On the contrary, endurance comes from the knowledge that God's Word *is never shackled* by cultural paradigm shifts or rampant unbelief. No matter the ministry landscape, we can take a stand, being willing to "suffer hardship even to imprisonment as a criminal; [knowing that] the word of God is not imprisoned" (2 Tim 2:9, NASB). Having spiritual stamina means that we "endure all things for the sake of those who are chosen, so that they also may obtain the salvation which is in Christ Jesus and with it eternal glory" (2 Tim 2:10, NASB). Sadly, ours is truly a generation who knows not Joseph.[3] The self-styled leaders of evangelicalism today are too disconnected from the heritage of godly leadership to understand that what they're crafting cannot sustain the people of God during what may prove to be the church's most embattled season of gospel ministry yet. Paul calls all generations of leaders to get in the flow of discipleship, accurately and faithfully passing the baton of gospel ministry to those who have demonstrated the gifts and commitment for lasting effectiveness.

WAR IS HARDSHIP

After I had completed Basic Training for the United States Air Force, I remember thinking, "Why did we have to endure Boot Camp?" Much of what we were forced to do there had nothing to do with our career field of choice. Military life thereafter was

---

3   The analogy here is based upon Exodus 1:8, where a new king ruled in Egypt who had no connection with the history of Joseph's character, widespread influence, and leadership integrity. Such disconnect resulted in faulty assumptions about Israel's history, national agenda, and divine purpose. Consequently, an adversarial posture was taken and generations suffered because of it. My point is that when leaders view their stewardship in a vacuum, the depth and consistency of spiritual influence loses its historical reference point.

much more relaxed, and once the initial training was over our superiors treated us like employees (with a few more rules of course). The marching, the sleepless nights, the yelling and screaming (and spitting!) were all behind me. So what was all the fuss about? The answer is very simple: The training is designed to test a person's mettle—the ability to *persevere under pressure*. Drill Instructors do everything to subject you to unbearable demands just to watch your response. There were constant inspections, long hours without adequate rest, relentless tension to meet the highest standards, hot and freezing conditions, endless study, no identity, minimal contact with the outside world, and a continual barrage of personal insults. If you can't learn to fight under these conditions, you'll never survive a real war! Some don't take it very seriously. Peacetime has lulled them to sleep and made them indifferent to the urgency of the training. Apathy, cowardice, and poor skills are among a soldier's most dangerous temptations. The deadly combination of all three signals the end of any successful battle plan. Like Timothy, we need a soldier's manual for a long and arduous campaign against the enemy of our souls!

Paul was realistic about the nature of the conflict: "No soldier in active service entangles himself in the affairs of everyday life, so that he may please the one who enlisted him a soldier" (2 Tim 2:4, NASB). Endurance comes from minimizing excess baggage and maximizing efforts to achieve God's battle objectives. I vividly recall breathing a sigh of relief upon my arrival at military Basic Training. An insider gave me a heads-up about bringing as little luggage as possible—only the barest essentials. I came with the clothes on my back and a scant number of toiletries. As drill sergeants rifled through our belongings during initial "shakedown," new recruits watched as radios, magazines, candy, family keepsakes, etc., were tossed in the garbage as useless. Anything of monetary or sentimental value was fair game. Not only were we systematically being cut off from civilian life and its comforts, but every potential hindrance to our becoming refined, chiseled military weapons was totally eliminated. This was radical transformation and singular focus!

One of the reasons men "burn out" in the service of Christ is the excess vanity and worldly distraction they simply refuse to jettison, which always leads to unfulfilled expectations. If we take on spiritual responsibility with designs on leisure, comfort, and perks, then we will not make enduring shepherds. Paul spoke of his own ministry in uncensored terms: "We are afflicted in every way … perplexed … persecuted … struck down … always carrying in the body the death of Jesus … . For we who live are always being given over to death for Jesus' sake" (2 Cor 4:8–11). God may not call us to the same severe trouble Paul experienced, but all truly effective leadership and ministry comes from maximum readiness for whatever God desires. Our affections cannot be "entangled." Pleasing "the one who enlisted [us]" must be our singular passion if we're going to enjoy the victories as well as endure the setbacks.

So where do we begin the housecleaning that will "disentangle" us for the long battle of spiritual leadership and responsibility? Well, here's an excess-baggage list to consider:

- sins of fear and worry about the cares of life—Christians like to take the edge off of Jesus' commands about worry by cleverly reclassifying this sin as "mild complaining" or "heartfelt concern." But sinful fear and worry is all about self-preservation! Worry cripples our ability to lead with *genuine concern* for the welfare of others because our thoughts are consumed with doubts about God's watchcare over us (Matt 6:25–34; Phil 4:6–7).

- inordinate attachment to possessions and comfort—When we are weighed down with controlling affections higher than Christ, it is impossible to make wise decisions in the face of leadership challenges (Matt 19:16–22; Luke 9:57–62; Col 3:1–4).

- unresolved bitterness—An unforgiving spirit always clouds our judgment as leaders. Others look to us for unbiased, biblical clarity in the battle for truth. Carrying around personal offenses will invite satanic deception, steal our joy, dull our convictions, and silence our effective witness (1 Cor 3:3–9; 2 Cor 2:10–11; Eph 4:29–32; Col 4:2–3).

- strong appetite for earthly amusements—While rest and wholesome entertainment are gifts from the Lord to be enjoyed, overexposure to such things quickly crowds responsibility at best, and cultivates a negative view of sober-minded, hard work at worst (Prov 6:6–11; Eccl 3:10; 4:5; 5:12; 10:18; 1 Cor 16:13; 1 Thess 4:11–12; 1 Pet 1:13; 5:8).

- fear of man—Godly and effective leadership demands that every allegiance be subordinated to the Lord Jesus Christ. Like the attachment to possessions and comfort, when other strong affections (e.g., family and friendships) capti-vate our hearts above our Master, we abdicate our privilege and responsibility to the manipulations and whims of oth-ers (Prov 3:5–6; 29:25; Luke 14:26–27).

A battle-ready soldier lives a very streamlined existence, desiring to please only the commander, and laying aside "every encumbrance and the sin which so easily entangles … [so that he might] run with endurance the race" (Heb 12:1, NASB).

WAR IS DISCIPLINE

No shortcuts! Paul says, "Also, if anyone competes as an athlete, he does not win the prize unless he competes according to the rules" (2 Tim 2:5, NASB). It is tragic when a superior athletic specimen fails to win the crown from disqualification or *lack of effort*! How many times have we seen gold medal-laden champions stripped of their crown after learning that they broke the rules of competition by using performance-enhancing drugs? Or what about gifted competitors whose work ethic habitually cuts corners? Paul's analogy of discipline in sports goes right to the heart of the matter. If you cheat or cut corners, the prize of effective leadership and ministry is forfeited. That's right. Paul speaks of "rules"—including cheating, but not exclusively in reference to dishonesty—primarily to underscore the importance of proper training. Paul was concerned that if leaders take shortcuts in their preparation and skill development, the work would suffer immeasurably.

In my high school years I was a competitive swimmer. I raced, played on our varsity water polo team, won a few trophies, and that was about the extent of my sports career. What frustrated me more than anything else was to see an athlete with extraordinary raw ability throwing such potential out the window in careless sloth. One particular student had everything a swimmer could want in sheer talent! His physique was long, with perfectly toned upper-body strength, and he was, as they say, "pure smoke" when he hit the water. In those years—during the mid-1970s—he was posting times as fast, or faster than some of the top Olympic swimmers for his events, and he was only a high school senior. The potential was of international proportions, and our coach knew it. But it was not to be. Mentors, teachers, friends, family members, and all who knew this young man tried desperately to help him envision what he could achieve. The problem was that he had no desire to put in the day-to-day hard work it would take. He was blessed with more talent than any one person should enjoy, but his heart was wrapped up in frivolous entertainments and carefree living. If he could win races with no discipline and minimal training, that was the life for him. Who knows what could have been? Perhaps Mark Spitz' amazing Olympic records would have fallen earlier than in the Michael Phelps era.

It is simply impossible to endure as a leader if you aren't willing to strenuously prepare and train "according to the rules." Using another sports analogy, Paul told the Corinthians that the

Christian life is a race we should run so as to win at all costs (1 Cor 9:24). His daily regimen included the exercise of "self-control in all things" and mortifying his passions to make them his slave rather than the other way around (1 Cor 9:25–27). Leaders cannot afford to take a vacation from the spiritual disciplines. Bible reading and study, prayer and fasting, evangelism, meditation, giving, spiritual service, and worship are the means given to us by God for the "Spirit-filled pursuit of Godliness."[4] Our enemy is constantly devising clever schemes intended to deceive and ultimately disqualify us (2 Cor 2:10–11; Eph 6:11–12). On our own we're no match against the demonic lies of hellish design, but by disciplining our lives for the purpose of advancing godliness (1 Tim 4:7) we can experience years of faithful, scandal-free ministry.

> O God my strength, how can I ever go the distance in these perilous times? With leaders compromising at every level, I see the necessity, the great urgency for shepherds who endure no matter the cost. I pray for Your abundant grace! Give me the courage to joyfully remain under the hardship and strain of leading Your people. May I never cut ministry corners in a foolish attempt to coddle my desire for ease and comfort. Help me to adorn, not tarnish, the tremendous legacy of faithfulness wrought by so many who have gone before. Amen.

---

4   Donald S. Whitney, *Spiritual Disciplines for the Christian Life* (Colorado Springs, CO: NavPress, 1991), 17. Whitney's very thorough treatment of the disciplines in this volume is extremely helpful, particularly his Chapters 2 and 3, entitled "Bible Intake" Parts 1 and 2.

PART
2

THE DANGERS
OF LEADERSHIP

6

LEADERS GOD RESISTS

No one would deny that immorality in the life of a spiritual leader is one of the most destructive forces encountered by God's people. The enemy loves to seduce leaders of low conviction into gross moral compromise, and he is tirelessly launching the careers of numerous counterfeit shepherds within the family of God who have no power over fleshly indulgence. When either scheme is successful the church suffers under years of broken trust and tainted witness. Indeed, sexual sin at the top, when discovered, instantly grinds ministry to a halt. Any church that has come through the terrible effects of immorality among its leaders knows the sudden devastation and years of suspicion that follow.

But what about those insidious, less dramatic diseases of character which mutate unnoticed and unchecked for years in a leader's life, yet equally ravage a healthy ministry? I'm referring to character flaws in a leader that are regularly ignored, deliberately neglected, and often masked with excuses. For example, the angry, quarrelsome leader stifles ministry under a cloud of intimidation and dominance. An insatiable desire for praise compels a leader to seek flattery on the one hand and jealously resist more gifted people on the other. A lust for power and control fills a leader with envy, selfish ambition, and greed. The sinful fear of man snares other leaders, making them suspicious of everyone and unwilling to be held accountable. Are these weaknesses any less damaging to the church than public moral scandal? Can a leader's self-will be overlooked and his leadership efforts continue to flourish? Will God smile on ministry efforts in spite of unchecked pride in a pastor?

The Scriptures severely warn that God hates pride, is opposed to prideful people, and extends lavish grace upon those who pursue humility (Ps 138:6; Prov 3:34; 6:17; 16:5, 18; Matt 23:12; Jas 4:6; 1 Pet 5:5). Pride *in a leader* required even stronger measures: "King Nebuchadnezzar, to you it is declared: sovereignty has been removed from you, and you will be driven away from mankind, and your dwelling place will be with the beasts of the field ... until you recognize that the Most High is ruler over the realm of mankind and bestows it on whomever He wishes" (Dan 4:31–32, NASB). The hypnotizing lure of power and preeminence snares many in positions of spiritual influence. What's worse is when leadership teams and elder boards do very little about these sins of the "natural born leader." A church's staff and congregation may endure years of belligerent, angry, defensive, and self-promoting leadership before the problem is openly discussed and dealt with. Quite often, when such men are confronted they retaliate in an attempt to save face, impugning all criticism as ungodly mutiny. God resists these leaders even if those around them retreat (Jas 4:6; 1 Pet 5:5).

Alexander Strauch speaks of the all-too-common pastor who has a "phenomenal knowledge of the Bible but who[se] ... theology [is] as clear as ice and twice as cold."[1] Faithful churches are often shredded by the insidious parasite of pride in a leader. What's to be done? How does a ministry guard against this crippling disease? Can a leader "keep [his] heart with all vigilance" (Prov 4:23) and thus avoid strangling effective gospel ministry? I believe he can, and through the clarity of Scripture he must! There are leaders whom God uses mightily and there are those He resists.

---

1   Alexander Strauch, *Leading with Love* (Littleton, CO: Lewis & Roth Publishers, 2006), 11.

THE BEGRUDGING LEADER

I've noticed that in the midst of serious ministry conflict, leaders can often become cynical, negative, and suspicious. When this happens, it's only a matter of time before the sheep become the target of a shepherd's frustration. This is the very opposite of Paul's long-term view of ministry: "I am again in the anguish of childbirth until Christ is formed in you!" (Gal 4:19). Compassion for the needs of others kept Paul from becoming a cynic; it kept him from teaching in harsh overtones; it prevented him from ministering like a man "trapped" by a responsibility he had no heart to do. Sometimes, the "pressure" felt by pastors to fulfill their "obligation" of shepherding can be surprisingly subtle. Men who have long since lost their joy and courage keep drudging on for fear of blemishing their reputation. *What will others think of me if I choose a different path?"* they may worry. *"Will I be seen as weak or unspiritual?"*

People-pleasing will quench the Spirit's influence over shepherding. In the flurry of ministry demands, a weary leader can become self-absorbed, no longer seeing God's purposes and under pressure to "perform" out of obligation. Have you ever "pressed forward" begrudgingly in the work of ministry in order to satisfy the expectations of a mentor, relative, or friend? I've known several men who entered seminary solely upon the enthusiastic designs of hopeful family members or to follow their ministry hero. Even fear of losing a steady paycheck has shackled some men to spiritual duties they weren't called to in the first place. A spiritual leader simply cannot serve both God and self!

First Peter 5:1–4 warns us to guard against a notorious band of sinister motives that rob the sheep of genuine care, the first of which (v. 2) declares that our leadership must never rise from a desire to preserve ourselves, to please others, or to impress the world. Leaders are to give oversight "not under compulsion, but willingly, as God would have you." We are called to serve the people of God from a deep burden to provide tender care after the fashion of the Chief Shepherd, and we are to do it with full sincerity! Just as the apostle Paul agonized over the desperate spiritual needs of God's flock (2 Cor 11:28–29; Gal 4:19; Col 1:28–2:1), so we must labor, not under a selfish sense of obligation or external pressure, but with the passion of a volunteer for the honor and glory of Jesus Christ. The work of spiritual leadership is not for the fainthearted, with its tireless demands, mental strain, and sobering divine accountability. Those who serve as if forced will be "incapable of genuine care"[2] and "will be unhappy, impatient, guilty, and ineffective."[3] Jesus warned of the cowardly hireling who skips town at the first sign of danger, leaving the flock to be devoured (John 10:12–13). If you're in it for fear of negative press, the approval of heroes, or simply to put a meal on the table, you qualify as a hireling. A man must be called to spiritual leadership, not coerced by some foreign ideal.[4]

Eliminating the leadership-out-of-obligation snare requires that we understand and identify with the plight of the human condition. Jesus, when He looked at the sea of humanity around him, saw people as "distressed and downcast, like sheep without a shepherd" (Matt 9:36, NASB). That's how we should see ourselves and others. Such conditions elicited our Lord's pity ("He felt compassion for them," v. 36, NASB) and urgent petition for gospel-laborers ("Therefore pray earnestly to the Lord of the harvest to send out laborers into his harvest," v. 38). When our

---

2   Alexander Strauch, *Biblical Eldership: An Urgent Call to Restore Biblical Church Leadership* (Littleton, CO: Lewis & Roth Publishers, 1986), 150.

3   Ibid.

4   In his exceptional book, *My Heart for Thy Cause* ([Fearn, Ross-shire, Great Britain: Christian Focus, 2002], 36–38), Brian Borgman offers a helpful summary of false reasons for assuming the role of spiritual leader in the church: (1) The pressure of a falsely (wrongly) instructed conscience; (2) The pressure of unwise and unsanctified ambitions of other people; (3) An unbalanced concept of spirituality; (4) An inaccurate assessment of one's gifts; (5) An unmet need for personal identity; (6) An inadequate view of the qualifications of the pastoral office; (7) An unmortified lust for authority, attention, influence, and monetary gain.

compassion for others in need wanes, our love for God has equally faded (1 John 3:17). Has the luster of your tender compassion lost its brilliance? Then you must repent and put yourself in the shoes of those you serve. Remember, we're all sheep! Another's struggle today was yours yesterday, or potentially will be yours tomorrow. The man whose heart longs to see Christ fully formed in God's people will bear the unselfish and tender marks of the Chief Shepherd, always willing to lay down his life for others.

THE GREEDY LEADER

Ah, Money! We desperately need it, we make everyday use of it, we try all kinds of trade secrets for stashing it away, and we often feel the sting of having misused it. Jesus spoke volumes about the use and potential abuse of money and possessions. John MacArthur's summary of the data is helpful:

> Sixteen of Christ's thirty-eight parables speak about how people should handle earthly treasure. In fact, our Lord taught more about such stewardship (one out of every ten verses in the Gospels) than about heaven and hell combined. The entire Bible contains more than two thousand references to wealth and property, twice as many as the total references to faith and prayer. What we do with the things God has given us is very important to Him.[5]

Money itself is amoral, but ruin and destruction await those who love it (1 Tim 6:9–10)! For those in spiritual leadership, the urgency of corralling materialism cannot be overemphasized. Again, Peter adds strong words about serving "eagerly" rather than "for shameful gain" (1 Pet 5:2). If begrudging leadership could be

---

5   John MacArthur, *Whose Money Is It Anyway? A Biblical Guide to Using God's Wealth* (Nashville, TN: Word Publishing, 2000), 3.

deemed "forced care," then serving to gain a profit is the worst kind of "false care"! Stated another way, where obligated service lacks *sincerity*, greedy service lacks *integrity*. Spiritual leadership becomes jealous, envious, spiteful, and partial when rooted in a desire for possessions at another's expense. A good shepherd—devoted and honest—looks to the needs of others and carefully uses resources for the good of all. Peter describes the Christlike leader as full of zeal for the highest spiritual ideals ("eagerly," 5:2—literally, a "devoted zeal to serve"), willing to make personal sacrifices wherever it is optimum for the flock.

Leaders in the church are frequently ensnared by the lure of riches, in spite of Paul's unmistakable link between greed and conceit: "As for the rich in this present age, charge them not to be haughty, nor to set their hopes on the uncertainty of riches, but on God, who richly provides us with everything to enjoy" (1 Tim 6:17). Pride and money-love go hand in hand. Big ministry, huge budgets, and cultural relevance can quickly inflate a leader's view of himself, making it difficult for anyone to challenge them with truth. How many churches have watched their once down-to-earth pastor morph into an aloof snob who can't be bothered with ministry needs because they cramp his book-signing schedule or weekly tee time? Dealing with this sin while surrounded by the temptations of a culture engrossed in materialism is challenging. It requires honest evaluation and a humble spirit to see our areas of weakness clearly. How do you know whether you lead with eagerness or greed? The following ten questions can help you get to the heart of it:

1. Are you a careful steward of your personal finances?

2. Do you faithfully, joyfully, and sacrificially give to the Lord's work?

3. Do you secretly resent the inconveniences of ministry because you "aren't paid enough for ministry beyond a normal work day"?

4. Do you find yourself befriending the more well-to-do folks in the congregation?

5. Are you easily consumed with worry and frustration over unforeseen financial trials?

6. Do you nervously hover over attendance and giving statistics?

7. Are you attracted to get-rich-quick schemes?

8. Does your ministry demonstrate a vulnerability to church growth fads?

9. How much do you talk about your material possessions and financial portfolios?

10. Does receiving gifts thrill you more than giving them?

All of the above areas signal the presence of materialistic interests. The love of money has so saturated Western culture that wanton avarice is no longer a vice but the single greatest virtue of the ambitious and executive. We are called instead to strive for wealth in "good works," and "to be generous and ready to share" (1 Tim 6:18). Spiritual leaders who are free from greed "go beyond minimal duty, self-interest, and money. They are creative and seek to give their best."[6]

THE BELLIGERENT LEADER

Aside from moral turpitude, there is hardly anything more incongruous and disgusting than domineering arrogance in a man called to be a tender and patient shepherd. To be blunt: the *faithful* spiritual leader does not use God-given privileges as a bludgeon. First Peter 5:3 is emphatic: "not domineering over those in your charge, but being examples to the flock." Leaders can quickly forfeit

6   Ibid., 151.

God's maximum blessing by falling under the spell of power over others. Strangely, there are great preachers who never seem to come under the weight of their own sermons! A masterful exposition on the humility of Christ's cross doesn't always result in the crucifixion of the preacher's pride. It is noteworthy that Peter contrasts a domineering leader with one whose example is worthy to be followed ("proving to be examples to the flock"—1 Pet 5:3, NASB). It is common knowledge that quarrelsome leaders care nothing about what they model. Their chief concern is control and intimidation, and when challenged, they loudly bring everyone in line to avoid facing their own inadequacies.

Robert G. Lee was, by the testimony of all who knew him, the very opposite of belligerent. He was a model shepherd whose ministry was marked by a "love for his people and a determined defense of the word of God."[7] Lee, born on November 11, 1886, in a South Carolina log cabin, was known not only for powerful preaching, but also for his rare blend of strong Bible exposition and *tender shepherding*. His view of ministry was simple: defend the truth and love others by helping them live it! This unadorned but thoroughly biblical approach resulted in a lifetime of extraordinary preaching and divine blessing.

Such effectiveness from such simplicity—how is that possible? The real secret lies in how Lee saw himself before a holy God:

> My own definition of the grace of God is this: the unlimited and unmerited favor given to the utterly undeserving. ... Sin is very powerful in this world. Sin is powerful as an opiate in the will. Sin is powerful as a frenzy in the imagination. Sin is powerful as a poison in the heart. Sin is powerful as a madness in the brain. Sin is powerful as a desert breath that drinks up all spiritual dews.

---

7   The Reformed Reader, "Baptist Cameos" 1999–2001, http://www.reformedreader.org/lee.htm (accessed August, 2005).

Sin is powerful as the sum of all terrors. Sin is powerful as the quintessence of all horrors. Sin is powerful
to devastate, to doom, to damn. ... No man can rescue
himself from the tyranny of sin. Men may reform, but
they cannot regenerate themselves. ... Regeneration is
the great change which God works in the soul when He
brings it into life ... . It is the change wrought ... when
pride is dethroned and humility enthroned; when passion is changed into meekness; when hatred, envy, and
malice are changed into a sincere and tender love for all
mankind. It is the change whereby the earthly, sensual,
devilish mind is turned into the mind that was in Christ.
The new birth is not the old nature altered, reformed, or
reinvigorated, but a being born from above.[8]

There is no more potent catalyst to a leader's usefulness
than a deep and abiding grasp of his rescue from deserved judgment! Lee was overwhelmed by an acute sense of his lost condition before God, and it energized his love for God's people. The
call to pastoral faithfulness is grounded in the purposes of God
for *His* people, requiring a full-range care that befits *His* design.
The trustworthy leader, then, will serve God best by feeding others with His food, reproving them with His Word, tending them
with His heart, and disciplining them with His grace. There is no
place in the church for pugnacious, quarrelsome, or angry leaders
(1 Tim 3:3; 2 Tim 2:24–25; 4:2). Do you manifest an attitude of
belligerence? Here's what to look for:

INTOLERANCE OF OTHERS

Some men simply can't hide their mounting frustration over the
shortcomings of others. Even small infractions are not acceptable

---

8   Ibid.

where a leader's reputation or convenience is threatened. You may not see yourself as an angry leader, but how you respond when people and circumstances do not cooperate tells the true story. A few years ago, I listened as a pastor confidently told of how he "stood for truth" in the midst of a recent and very ugly church split. He had been the pastor for several years and was becoming increasingly resentful that his congregation frequently grumbled at his teaching and leadership. Why had they not appreciated his ministry? Where was the willing submission commanded in Scripture? One Sunday, his frustration resulted in a public display of anger during the worship service. Such behavior shocked the church, and eventually precipitated his dismissal. Sadly, the absence of character formation in others exposed a glaring flaw in his own maturity, crippling any potential ministry he may have had in their lives. Had he remembered that Christlike shepherding requires patience and kindness, especially when wronged (2 Tim 2:24), the Word of God would not have been maligned. All Christians must learn to bear with one another's weaknesses, but leaders are called to a greater forbearance and compassion than those we lead. An intolerant shepherd may be free to carry out his ministry for a season, but God resists such attitudes and will most certainly chasten an impatient leader severely until he faces the problem.

ARROGANCE AND JOYLESSNESS

Angry leaders reveal that they have a personal agenda which resists the sovereign purposes of God. More to the point, harsh leaders refuse to acknowledge God's use of trials *for their good and His glory*. As James 1:2–4 commands, "Consider it all joy, my brethren, when you encounter various trials, knowing that the testing of your faith produces endurance. And let endurance have its perfect result, that you may be perfect and complete, lacking in nothing" (NASB). Indeed, the weaknesses, idiosyncrasies, and shortcomings of others are used by God to reveal areas where we desperately need work. God often puts someone in our path whose immaturities test our patience and commitment to sacrificially love them as Christ has loved us. Intolerance of others reveals our lack of love and forbearance, which, according to Scripture, instantly turns their sin into a secondary concern (Matt 7:1–4).

In a sermon, one preacher captured the heart behind anger with this assertion: "Anger is the opposite of love because anger says, 'I matter so much, if you do something that I don't like, I'm going to let you have it.'"[9] On a much more frightening scale, when we're angry at people and circumstances, we are really lashing out at God's good providence. Instead of kissing the hand that afflicts us, we're demanding that God order our lives by our script, our assessment of people, our comfort level. How often on the one hand have we boldly asserted that we "are not [our] own, for [we] were bought with a price" (1 Cor 6:19–20), while on the other behaving as though the Lord has no right over us? Unchecked arrogance at this level quickly drains the joy and blessing out of ministry.

The remedy is given at length in Chapter 3, but I'll summarize it again: all arrogance is shattered under the powerful display of humility at the cross of Jesus Christ (Phil 2:3–8). The cross proves—in spite of our personal claim to inherent worthiness and value—that it is Christ alone who is worthy; He is the treasure of highest value. In a word, He matters, not us! In the grand scheme of redemption, it is due to the grandeur of His love, the wonder of His grace, and the "kind intention of His will" (Eph 1:5, NASB) that we matter at all. When we lead others with such truth as the backdrop, no matter how challenging, arrogance dies a natural death. As Jim Shaddix has poignantly stated regarding pastoral leadership, "Preacher, if your preaching is constantly calling

---

9   John MacArthur, "Perfect Love: The Qualities of True Love," sermon transcript, http://www. biblebb.com/files/MAC/sg1865.htm (accessed March 31, 2009).

people's attention to the crucified life, then those of us who listen to you will not have time to sing your praises."[10]

SELF-RIGHTEOUSNESS AND JUDGMENTAL ATTITUDES

Another evil that plagues the belligerent leader is self-righteousness—amplifying everyone else's sin while minimizing his own. It's the age-old "log in the eye" hypocrisy Jesus warned against in Matthew 7:1–4. This is dangerous ground to tread! God is as direct as ever regarding His severe response to this ugly pretension. Jesus says, "Judge not, that you be not judged. For with the judgment you pronounce you will be judged, and with the measure you use it will be measured to you" (Matt 7:1–2). When we look down on others with haughty judgment, we invoke the same compassionless treatment from God toward our infirmities. What a terrifying response from the living God! Belligerent people are told they can expect to be handled by God, not according to His tender compassion, but with a severity matching their contempt of others. Such words should sober even the most hardened heart, and result in a fresh realization that self-righteousness tops God's list of man's most despised iniquities (Prov 6:16–19).

I've also found that self-righteousness and outbursts of anger go together like chips and salsa! Every self-promoting leader I've known is pushy, easily provoked, prone to bitterness, and unforgiving. Such pride is never open to critique and won't tolerate a rebuke. Negligently, some leaders try to "clear the air" by generally admitting to a quick temper, or by making regular verbal apologies for offenses without the hard work of serious character reformation. This is a profound danger to one's spiritual integrity and conscience. Proverbs 28:13 teaches that shallow, half-hearted apologies invite more trouble, while an honest confession and

---

10   Jim Shaddix, *The Passion-Driven Sermon* (Nashville, TN: Broadman & Holman Publishers, 2003), 35.

desire to forsake sin stirs up compassion. An explosive temper is not a *minor drawback* that others must learn to endure until it's over. Proverbs 19:19 states, "A man of great anger will bear the penalty, for if you rescue him, you will only have to do it again." Anger problems do not simply dissipate over time. That's because lurking behind angry tantrums are the ugly idols of reputation, personal rights, and revenge. Bitterness and anger say, "I deserve to be treated as I please; my reputation matters most; my expectations will be met, or else!"

Some leaders regularly pay homage to their own reputation rather than living for the exaltation of Jesus Christ. They uphold a set of personal rights and expectations for others to acknowledge and serve. Martha Peace has unmasked this self-orientation well: "One way we weave God into our self-focus is by having a self-focused view of the universe. Being overly taken with our own importance, we try to obligate God to grant our wishes and make us feel special."[11] Human beings obligating God? What a ridiculous notion! Yet, that is precisely what drives many leaders' perception of themselves. When violated, a belligerent leader satisfies his appetite for revenge in a volcanic tirade, hoping to make someone pay. If these idols of self-worship are not smashed with a vigorous repentance and mind renewal, a trail of broken relationships, destroyed credibility, and lifeless ministry will result! Our only hope is to cultivate an insatiable appetite for Christ over every other desire. There's probably no greater description of this reality than the words of the great Scottish pastor/theologian, Thomas Chalmers:

> We only cease to be the slave of one appetite because another taste has brought it into subordination. A youth may cease to idolize sensual pleasure, but it's only because the idol of material gain has gotten the ascendancy. There

11   Martha Peace, *Attitudes of a Transformed Heart* (Bemidji, MN: Focus Publishing, 2002), 147.

is not one personal transformation in which the heart is left without an object of beauty and joy. Its desire for one particular object may be conquered, but its desire to have some object is unconquerable. The only way to dispossess the heart of an old affection is by the expulsive power of a new one.[12]

For believers, the "expulsive power" has to be a Spirit-controlled, unquenchable thirst for the glory of the Lord Jesus Christ. If you're steeped in habitual condescension toward others, flee with great haste to the mercy of God that He might arouse a new passion to lead for the exaltation of the Savior.

CONCEIT AND INSECURITY

In Romans 12:3, the apostle Paul urgently warns us never to think more highly of ourselves than is fitting for a sinner saved by grace. When we become intoxicated with our own gifts and influence we begin to see people as a means to our advancement. Today's leaders seem so much more easily seduced by the lure of public recognition, wealth, power, sensuality, and personal significance. Conceit and lust for significance are graphically portrayed in a man named Diotrephes, mentioned in 3 John 9–10. His ministry is the classic account of a leader for whom God's people became a personal trophy. He had allowed his heart to drift into the treacherous waters of pride and conceit, seduced by the influence of personal power and human praise.

Diotrephes was a church leader of some notable responsibility, probably a senior pastor by today's standards. For all his achievements in ministry he is described in Scripture as an

---

12   Adam Philip, *Thomas Chalmers: Sermons and Writings*, Discourse 9, "The Expulsive Power of a New Affection," http://www.newble.co.uk/chalmers/comm9.html (accessed October, 2007).

egocentric personality who "[loved] to be first among them" (3 John 9, NASB). He had an insatiable desire for preeminence. His heart secretly delighted in the praises of others, which fed his exalted view of his own abilities. When a leader satisfies himself with the cheers of men, he lays the groundwork for a host of ministry-disrupting behaviors. For example, Diotrephes' love for preeminence led to an unsubmissive heart toward church authority (3 John 9). Furthermore, he became deceitful, "unjustly accusing [John] with wicked words" (v. 10, NASB). Egocentric leadership is always intolerant and hyper-critical of others. When such sinful habits get a hold of our hearts, we position ourselves for maximum attention and readily dispense with another's ministry gifts, talents, and ideas. Like Diotrephes, we won't tolerate anyone encroaching upon our territory.

An appetite for man's applause signals ingratitude for the gifts God has given and a desire for significance outside of God's will. The Scriptures warn against "seek[ing] one's own glory" (Prov 25:27; 28:6–7). We can avoid the lure of man's praise by remembering that our significance is found in becoming useful to Christ. Moreover, we are told in 1 Peter 4:10 that we have "received" spiritual gifts from God and are merely "stewards of God's varied grace." Apart from Him we can accomplish nothing! How can you know whether you love the praises of men? A few simple questions may help: Do you withhold praise from others? Do you delight in getting attention? Are you uncomfortable in the presence of gifted peers? Would others describe you as self-promoting?[13] If you struggle to rejoice in the usefulness of others, you have laid the seedbed for cultivating a love of praise.

Equally destructive was Diotrephes' lust for power, which always leads to isolation from those authorities to whom we are

---

13 It is healthy to ask for a critique from those under your leadership. Often a person's opportunism is excused as a "strong leadership quality." The Scriptures teach, however, that strong leaders accentuate the usefulness of others and enjoy seeing someone else receive honor for faithful service (1 Cor 3:5–7). Beware the man who boasts of his own gifts (Prov 25:14).

accountable.[14] Diotrephes opposed John's apostolic leadership because he viewed others as obstacles to the furtherance of his own power and control. Verse 10 (NASB) says he was "not satisfied with" mere slander, but also tried to hinder the outreach ministries of other churches. In his resentment he refused to serve a traveling band of missionaries ("he ... does not receive the brethren"). If we love control we will be suspicious of others for fear of losing ground in the battle for self-importance. Scripture teaches that we are never to shepherd "as lording it over those allotted to [our] charge" (1 Pet 5:3, NASB).

The sheep are a *delegated* responsibility from the Chief Shepherd to whom we shall give an account.[15] When a leader does not tremble at the very thought of accountability to Christ, he is left to his petty intimidations and oppressive tactics. Anyone who stood against Diotrephes became a target of his bitterness. He manipulated his own congregation, incited them to disfellowship with anyone who went against his orders. This is not leadership but personal domination! How can you know whether you have fallen into the power-hungry trap? Examine your life and look for the following evidences:

- viewing others as a threat to your success—Are you comfortable around gifted peers? Some leaders burn huge amounts of energy trying to keep others from succeeding. They sinfully fear that God may grant tremendous influence to other leaders, which detracts from their own.

- unteachable when contradicted—When you're hungry for the rush of power over others, you will be compelled to

---

14   Proverbs 18:1 teaches that all who isolate themselves and resist sound counsel are consumed with their own desires.

15   Hebrews 13:17 is a similar passage which clearly refers to pastoral accountability, but includes the idea that such a responsibility should be a joy.

shut down any critique whether true or false. Unteachable leaders ground their influence in intimidation rather than humble service.

- letting others bear the blame for failed decisions—Controlling leaders can never admit wrong, so they happily take credit for successes while pointing at others when failure comes. Since "respect" is viewed as something the leader demands from his people, then failure is seen as weakness and therefore should not be traced back to the top of the pile.

- withholding important resources and information needed by others—Power-mongers know that information is a major key to controlling others, so they obsess over the transfer and communication of these vital resources. Do you hoard what others critically need to reach institutional goals? Are you honest and upfront about what you know and don't know so that the greatest benefit will be accomplished through the collaborative efforts of everyone?

- unwilling to delegate responsibility—Wanting power and control makes us fearful that our reputation may suffer when others fail, or jealous that someone else may be appreciated above ourselves.

These are the marks of conceited and sinfully fearful leadership. Ruthlessly identify them in yourself, plead with God for His grace to discern their root affections, and saturate your mind and heart with every truth against them that proceeds out of the mouth of God!

Father in heaven, it is frightening to think that You would resist my ministry efforts. I need a fresh glimpse of my responsibilities through the eyes of the Chief Shepherd. Strengthen me for the hard work of mortifying pride, materialism, selfish ambition, and belligerence. May I never lead begrudgingly; may I continually shed the covetous longings in my heart for a more lucrative, comfortable life. When I become harsh and lead with intimidation, reprove me swiftly with thoughts of Christ's cross that it might sober my judgment. I confess that I am but an instrument in Your hands, and that You alone can make me useful. Amen.

7

DESPISING THE GIFTS

The Corinthian church had severe problems! If our congregation received a letter like the one Paul delivered to Corinth, we might be tempted to simply turn out the lights, close the doors behind us, and pray for mercy. It's hard to imagine a ministry more steeped in the kind of sins that easily destroy churches. They were dealing with everything from bitter factions to leadership personality cults to gross immorality (including incest) to lawsuits against one another. Marriages were fouled up, Christian liberties were being horribly abused, and their love feasts brought out the worst kinds of hypocrisy, self-indulgence, and trampling of the poor. Frankly, that the Corinthian assembly was still together at the time of Paul's letter is astonishing.

A diverse and highly gifted congregation (1 Cor 1:7), Corinth struggled to understand that without a deep and Spirit-controlled love for one another, all the talent and giftedness in the world will not produce effective gospel ministry. Though the plain text of 1 Corinthians 13:1–3 cannot be improved upon, Alexander Strauch's rather blunt paraphrase is appropriate:

> If I were the most gifted communicator to ever preach, so that millions of people were moved by my oratory, but didn't have love, I would be an annoying, empty wind-bag before God and people. If I had the most charismatic

personality, so that everyone was drawn to me like a powerful magnet, but didn't have Christlike love, I would be a phony, a dud. If I were the greatest visionary leader the church has ever heard, but didn't have love, I would be misguided and lost. If I were the bestselling author on theology and church growth, but didn't have love, I would be an empty-headed failure. If I sacrificially gave all my waking hours to discipling future leaders, but did it without love, I would be a false guide and model.[1]

The Corinthians habitually used their spiritual gifts for self-promotion rather than to edify others. The grace-gifts of the Spirit are given to the church to build up the saints. These enablements, however, are often the breeding ground for the grossest kinds of jealousy and self-exaltation.

SLAVES AND KINGS

One of my favorite passages in all Scripture is the thirtieth chapter of Proverbs. It is jam-packed with wisdom. My youngest son has often joked that verse 2 would make a great "life-verse" for the teen years: "Surely I am more stupid than any man, and I do not have the understanding of a man" (NASB). And then there's the stunning prayer of verses 8 and 9, where Agur asks for just enough in life that he would never be tempted to dishonor God. And who doesn't chuckle at the word picture in verse 15, using "leech" to vividly depict the heart that selfishly consumes. Some years back I was reading through it again, and suddenly verses 21–23 flashed in neon: "Under three things the earth trembles; under four it cannot bear up: a slave when he becomes a king, and a fool when he is filled with food, an unloved woman when she gets a husband, and a maidservant when she displaces her mistress." It was the

1   Alexander Strauch, *Leading with Love* (Littleton, CO: Lewis & Roth Publishers, 2006), 16.

first in the list of illustrations that caught my eye. When a slave is suddenly given absolute power, the inevitable result is destructive consumption! Why? Because an impoverished and jealous peasant longing for palace life cannot handle the gravity of kingly responsibility. The less privileged are tempted to resent anyone who has more, and if given the opportunity to ascend from the street to the throne, they would abuse the power in fits of irresponsible excess.

The text became a fitting analogy to what happened in Corinth. Those whose gifts were less public in their operation resented the gifts of greater notoriety, causing them to clamor for the "showy gifts" where the Spirit had not bestowed them. And the more publicly gifted believers looked down on others who labored behind the scenes. They were all like so many immature slaves, turning royal privilege into a playground of power and pre-eminence, and enviously clawing for fame and reputation in the church. The ministry trembled beneath their unbridled pride, and the result was disastrous! Some were standing up in the assembly trying to speak for God without a Spirit-enabled gift to do so (1 Cor 12:3; 14:37–38); others were using their gifts to "show off" rather than edify the church (1 Cor 14:12–19, 26); women were usurping the role of male leadership by wanting recognition for their intelligence and ability to teach (1 Cor 14:34–35); and the less public gifts of the Spirit were considered inconsequential (1 Cor 12:12–16). As Strauch pointed out, they were missing the twin principles of love and mutual edification. Whatever your spiritual giftedness, you cannot edify the church without ministering with love and humility!

While on staff at a large church where a seminary resides, I would regularly meet with students for leadership development. A primary caution I would repeat to them was the need to ferociously guard their hearts from gift-envy. Because of my role at the church, students would often ask for opportunities to be mentored and to help me with my responsibilities, for which I was exceedingly grateful. Frequently, however, what some students really wanted was an official staff position—"ministry director" or "pastoral resident"—a title that gave them authority and status. They claimed a desire to serve wherever needed, but they secretly longed for others to see them as gifted and intelligent. What they needed most was to be tested. I would offer them unvarnished tasks usually associated with the non-public serving gifts to see if their heart was impartial. Such ministry proved too insignificant for one young man who became frustrated at my unwillingness to recognize his obvious gifts. He hurriedly went from one staffer to the next looking for anyone who had discernment enough to see his unappreciated skills. The ever-wise Charles Spurgeon tells the humorous story of a similar occasion at his Pastors' College. It is worth quoting at length:

> One young gentleman with whose presence I was once honoured, has left on my mind the photograph of his exquisite self. ... He sent word into my vestry one Sabbath morning that he must see me at once. His audacity admitted him; and when he was before me he said, "Sir, I want to enter your College, and should like to enter it at once." "Well Sir," said I, "I fear we have no room for you at present, but your case shall be considered." "But mine is a very remarkable case, Sir; you have probably never received such an application as mine before."[2]

Spurgeon indulged the student's taste for parading his gifts, and gave him an appointment the following Monday. The trap was set and Spurgeon seemed delighted to be playing a part in the young man's upcoming lesson in humility. The shrewd preacher recorded the encounter:

---

2   C. H. Spurgeon, *Lectures to My Students* (Grand Rapids, MI: Zondervan Publishing House, 1954), 38.

[The applicant] came on the Monday bringing with him the questions, answered in a most extraordinary manner. As to books, he claimed to have read all ancient and modern literature, and after giving an immense list he added, "This is but a selection; I have read most extensively in all departments." As to his preaching, he could produce the highest testimonials, but hardly thought they would be needed, as a personal interview would convince me of his ability at once. His surprise was great when I said, "Sir, I am obliged to tell you that I cannot receive you." "Why not, Sir?" "I will tell you plainly. You are so dreadfully clever that I could not insult you by receiving you into our College, where we have none but rather ordinary men; the president, tutors, and students, are all men of moderate attainments, and you would have to condescend too much in coming among us."[3]

I love Spurgeon's unmatched sense of irony! Undaunted, the upstart wouldn't be denied and challenged the Prince of Preachers to select any text or subject, upon which he would speak impromptu and amaze his hearers. Spurgeon said, "No, thank you, I would rather not have the trouble of listening to you."[4] The student replied, "Trouble, Sir! I assure you it would be the greatest possible pleasure you could have."[5] The student's arrogance, if it weren't so hideous, would be laughable! Spurgeon ends the story with these telling words, "The gentleman was unknown to me at the time, but he has since figured in the police court as too clever by half."[6] We're not surprised that self-promotion goes

---

3   Ibid.

4   Ibid.

5   Ibid., 38–39.

6   Ibid., 39.

hand in hand with a disdain for authority. One young associate pastor told me that he was "born to preach." Well, perhaps, but wisdom warns, "Let another praise you, and not your own mouth; a stranger, and not your own lips" (Prov 27:2).

MISPLACED MINISTERS

I have also been delighted, on the other hand, to find many aspiring shepherds who sought only the Lord's affirmation and leading for their ministry future. They weren't looking for a place to trumpet their gifts, but rather opportunities to test their character. Nor had they already determined the unique place their gifts would take them in the work of the church. This is an important lesson to learn early on in our preparation for leadership. First Corinthians 12:18 says, "But as it is, God arranged the members in the body, each one of them, as He chose." The same point is raised in verse 24, stating clearly that God, not man, has composed the body according to His design.

I'm grieved that today's evangelical culture, with its insatiable appetite for larger venues, bigger budgets, and manufactured influence has bred the same spirit of pride and envy over the gifts. Those who have exceptional teaching and leading abilities are quickly and publicly elevated to celebrity status, often before their character has been sufficiently tested for such responsibility. Indeed, it seems that the faster and more controversial one's rise to public fame, the greater honor and wider influence over the hearts and minds of believers is freely given. Evangelicalism seems intoxicated with the speaking and leading gifts, with thousands lining up to register for conference after endless conference regardless of a ministry celebrity's questionable character. And yet, for those whose spiritual gifts impact the church without public fanfare, honorable mention is rarely garnered in the flowchart of most church growth strategies. This is completely backward from the way God intends the church to operate.

THE DANGER OF DEFORMITY

The body of Christ is a wonder of diverse gifts and callings, all brought together for the purpose of reflecting the beauty, unity, and symmetry of our glorious Redeemer. When we allow sinful desires and perspectives to rule hearts, the body becomes twisted, deformed, and unable to function properly. I have a long-time friend who suffered severe physical injuries during a traffic accident in his youth. He's always been grateful for the Lord's kindness to him for letting him live, but the physical problems haven't been easy. His legs don't work properly, and he has a terrible time trying to communicate due to subsequent strokes. It can be frustrating when the human body's design malfunctions. One misfiring part of the body greatly affects others, deforming the God-intended unity of motion and function. The church can suffer the same trouble when her members begin to operate as if isolated from the rest, or when one behaves as if primary.

To be specific, if you serve the church with speaking gifts, you must reject the idea that you're indispensable, and that the body of Christ is primarily made up of orators. Or perhaps your gifts are of the less noticed, service-type. You must forsake all jealous desires for different gifts, and you should resist thinking that you're not necessary to the Lord's work. Paul says these attitudes cause the body to become deformed and grotesque (1 Cor 12:17, 19). It is wrong to conclude that the church can do without your faithful ministry. It is amazing to me how many good deacons try desperately to be elders because they've concluded that there's greater impact or status at the elder level. The result is a person carrying leadership burdens he was never gifted to bear, while the need for godly deacons goes unmet. First Corinthians 12:15–19 teaches believers the proper way to view our strengths and limitations:

> If the foot should say, "Because I am not a hand, I do not belong to the body," that would not make it any less

a part of the body. And if the ear should say, "Because I am not an eye, I do not belong to the body," that would not make it any less a part of the body. If the whole body were an eye, where would be the sense of hearing? If the whole body were an ear, where would be the sense of smell? But as it is, God arranged the members in the body, each one of them, as he chose. If all were a single member, where would the body be?

All the gifts given by the Spirit are crucial and necessary for the majesty of Jesus Christ to be manifested. Unhappily, there are those in the church whose gifts have been so carelessly minimized that they've completely stalled in their zeal and service. Scripture teaches that everyone ought to *enjoy the sense of their usefulness* in the ministry (1 Cor 12:23–25), and that the body must never have an unwritten "pecking order" of the gifts. Preaching, of course, should always be given the priority when it comes to the corporate assembly and doctrinal instruction, but no gift should be treated as either exalted and isolated or second-class and inconsequential. Such misuse of the Spirit's grace is an affront to God, who composed the body exactly as His perfect wisdom demands.

As leaders, we have to be brutally honest with ourselves. Are we clawing after the more noticed gifts and leadership roles? Where do our gifts best fit in the purposes of God for the advance of the gospel? Are we content with our strengths for ministry and the special niche the Holy Spirit has carved out for our life? All believers, but especially those in leadership, ought to do the ministry a favor and bloom where God plants us. If you're gifted to teach but lack shepherding qualities, be a faithful teacher in the church and *stay away from the pastorate.* I know so many gifted teachers who leave their staffers and congregation members floundering because they simply won't acknowledge that shepherding is not their strong suit. Be content to let others use their gifts where you are lacking.

Perhaps you have strong evangelistic gifts but spend most of your time frustrated in some administrative capacity. Leave the nuts and bolts to those who delight in those things, and ask the ministry to send you out as a church planter. I've watched people with mercy gifts become stifled trying to organize events instead of visiting the sick and needy. Perhaps your gifts are suited to administrative management (1 Cor 12:28—"administrations" or "steering") but you're limited when it comes to leading with great faith and vision. Don't imagine that the rudder of the ship is somehow less significant than the captain. Let those with gifts of faith and leadership offset your weaker areas while you are fruitful in your strengths. This is how the body operates in harmony. People with helping gifts should be placed where the ministry is fainthearted and always struggling to get things accomplished. Specially-graced givers should be provided with a list of needs to meet and pray for. Have you ever noticed that gifted exhorters aren't as effective by the bedside of the infirmed, but put them with the weary and the strength of the work quickly returns. The mercy gifts struggle to flourish where extraordinary courage is required, but where healing is needed, they shine.

All of us, from time to time, may be asked to serve in areas we're not gifted for, or where someone more gifted would have greater impact. It's an honor to be asked, and with the Lord's help, regardless of our limitations, we can be a servant to bless that ministry as long as needed until a more effective person is raised up. In general, however, those who know their blend of spiritual gifting should strive to serve the body in those special capacities. Teachers should spend their energies teaching, leaders should lead, exhorters should exhort; servers, helpers, givers, and the merciful should labor with all their might where those gifts thrive; and all the gifts, however unique, must operate, not for man's applause, but for God's glory! Someone may ask, "What if I have gifts in multiple areas?" Well, the Spirit gives each of us a unique mix of enablements, perfectly tailored for the building up of the body in love (Eph 4:16). Some individuals manifest a blend of several *types* of gifts. Such uniqueness is according to the Lord's purposes. The point of this chapter, and the weakness most glaring in the multi-gifted congregation at Corinth, is the danger of despising a gift in jealousy and envy.

THE BEAUTY OF BALANCE

The church is greatly harmed when certain gifts are elevated and others are neglected or minimized. There should be balance in the body which reflects the beauty of Christ! In fact, the public gifts (e.g., preaching, teaching, leading), which tend to elicit greater corporate admiration, are not worthy of more honor at all. Scripture says,

> The eye cannot say to the hand, "I have no need of you," nor again the head to the feet, "I have no need of you." On the contrary, the parts of the body that seem to be weaker are indispensable, and on those parts of the body that we think less honorable we bestow the greater honor, and our unpresentable parts are treated with greater modesty, which our more presentable parts do not require. But God has so composed the body, giving greater honor to the part that lacked it, that there may be no division in the body, but that the members may have the same care for one another. (1 Cor 12:21–25)

The truth here is so simple, yet profoundly practical. Paul tells us that God has composed the body with gifts that stand out and those that are more modest—the "presentable" and "unpresentable" parts. When our selfishness and pride get into the mix, we exalt the gifts that make us look good to others, while neglecting the honor of more modest giftedness. Yet, God intends for the "presentable" people to lovingly and gratefully *bestow greater honor* on those gifts that we normally deem "unpresentable." In other words, the non-public, behind-the-scenes, serving gifts, which sacrificially grace the body day after day, should be upheld as desperately vital to the strength of the ministry by those who already enjoy the public notice of their usefulness. What a wise plan from the heart of God! Every believer is crucial to the work, but some have gifts that are best designed for use where no one else sees. They are the ones often grossly neglected while the church is busy chattering about people of more "showy" impact. We are commanded to do the very opposite. If your gifts, being more public, are naturally honored, it should be your delight to transfer that honor to others who have been used by God to build you up in the faith. If someone mentions the blessings of your ministry, be thankful, but use it as a personal reminder to express gratitude to the many others who've made your labor possible. It is right to offer up grateful praise for the countless ways God uses others to minister to us. Elaborating on this kind of interdependence, John MacArthur states,

> Even as Christians we sometimes fall prey to the notion that, because we are complete in Christ and because He is our sufficiency, we therefore do not really need anyone else to live a faithful Christian life. Yet the idea completely contradicts Scripture. God has made us and redeemed us not only for Himself but for each other. We would never have heard of God or of the gospel had it not been for someone leading us to Christ or providing material for us to read. We could not have grown in faith and obedience had it not been for Christian teachers and friends who helped us and guided us. We cannot possibly fulfill our own ministry, whatever it is, without being mutually dependent on others.[7]

---

7   John MacArthur, *The MacArthur New Testament Commentary: 1 Corinthians* (Chicago, IL: Moody Press, 1996), 318.

How marvelous it is when God's people begin to care for one another as God intended. Leaders should learn to be conscientious, frequently thanking others in public and in private for their faithful service. I served under Dr. MacArthur's ministry for many years, and I can attest firsthand to his caring practice of the interdependence principle. No matter what leadership issues or ministry battles were going on privately, his public expressions about the ministry were filled with the deepest gratitude for his fellow elders, the congregation, and the privileges of gospel ministry. Never once from the pulpit did I hear a negative tone about the ministry, nor did I ever observe in private any condescension toward the different gifting of others. Such a consistent example has had a profound effect on my life and ministry. Arrogance and gift-mongering have no place in the body of Christ, especially among leaders. Love, compassion, and humility bring balance to the operation of the gifts, and where such qualities reign, pride cannot gain any ground (1 Cor 12:26).

> *Dear God, how often I have wanted the applause of men. One moment I'm content with how You've gifted me, and the next I'm either using my abilities for self-exaltation or envying the giftedness and impact of others. Oh, how I need daily reminders of the many ways I've been undeservedly blessed through the body of Christ. Show me my limitations and weaknesses frequently enough that my strengths are seen in proper context. Amen.*

8

CRITICISM

Everyone, without exception, has faced a harsh critic or two. For those in leadership, the target on our backs is much larger than for other roles, making criticism—the helpful and the nasty—one of the most hazardous and potentially hurtful challenges a leader will face. It comes in all forms, and often without warning. It can be as mild as a simple misunderstanding, or as severe as personal slander with malicious intent. Curtis Thomas lends his practical insights to the inevitability of criticism:

> [Complaints] will come from those who are often unhappy and simply have a complaining spirit. Others will present complaints regarding matters about which they have little information and that they have not thought through to any degree. Others will be attempting to help us in our walk, teaching, administration, or leadership. Some will be good suggestions and should not be considered complaints. These should be welcomed and used beneficially. Some will come with hostile attitudes, and others will be brought to us with a very gentle spirit. But they will come ... . They are a fact of church life.[1]

---

1   Curtis C. Thomas, *Practical Wisdom for Pastors: Words of Encouragement and Counsel for a Lifetime of Ministry* (Wheaton, IL: Crossway Books, 2001), 123–24.

On one occasion, while on my way to teach a Bible class at church, a man stopped me and said, "I've been bitter at you for the last four years." I was shocked! I hadn't had a negative thought about this person for as long as I had known him. Obviously stunned, I asked, "What in the world did I do to offend you?" I'll never forget his answer: "I said 'hello' to you one morning in passing and you never responded." For some, that's all it takes to hatch a serious criticism. Thankfully, we were able to be restored, and the man even acknowledged his lack of love in holding a long-term grudge over a misguided perception. Not all offenses and criticisms end so positively. But handling any criticism with wisdom and patience is essential to godly and effective leadership. Alexander Strauch rightly notes the urgency: "A lack of patience in a Christian leader is a serious deficiency. An impatient leader is as destructive to people as an impatient father is to his children or as an impatient shepherd is to his sheep."[2] No one likes to be criticized. No one! But spiritual leaders are called to respond in a biblical manner regardless of the source. A critic may be "all wet," or they may be right on target; either way we must learn how to use criticism to our leadership advantage.

LEARNING HOW TO LISTEN

A number of years ago, while working for a large military defense contracting company, I would often cross paths with the CEO's top chauffer, "Joe." He was a comical little figure who never seemed to notice anything that was going on around him. My co-workers often joked that if you told "Joe" any bit of information, no matter how dire, he would probably respond with "great, great, that's great" and move along unaffected. One day I decided to test this theory with my co-workers watching via security camera. I met "Joe" in the elevator and said "hello." Still looking down, he

---

2   Alexander Strauch, *Leading With Love* (Littleton, CO: Lewis & Roth Publishers, 2006), 42.

responded, "How ya doin'?" I quickly replied, "Well, my mother and father were both killed recently in a car accident!" Without missing a beat, "Joe" said, "Great, great, that's wonderful." My family and I have laughed over that incident for years because it illustrates how self-absorbed and distracted people can be when someone is trying to communicate what's on his mind and heart. How often have you "heard" what someone said and moments later had no idea of the content? What about times when we're already formulating an answer long before someone has finished expressing his burden? Facing criticism well requires undistracted and careful listening. It's not easy, but the Scriptures command leaders to model how it's done (2 Tim 2:24–26).

GENUINE INTEREST

Listening is not simply "hearing," but involves receiving with *genuine interest* all that is being communicated. In my experience a lot of criticism can be diffused before it becomes ugly by the simple practice of skilled listening. When a criticism is offered, our natural reaction is to become defensive, looking for all the reasons why that person has both misunderstood our intentions and misconstrued the facts. Defensiveness, however, clouds our judgment and our perspectives suddenly become subjective and self-oriented. A defensive posture is all about self-preservation and never leads to genuine interest and care for the welfare of others. If you believe a criticism to be false, you must be patient, listening carefully to the heart behind what is being said. James 1:19 says, "Let every person be quick to hear, slow to speak" and Proverbs 18:13 is even more pointed: "If one gives an answer before he hears, it is his folly and shame." Being genuinely interested requires the discipline of self-control. Leaders should be concerned, not for their own comfort and ease, but for the spiritual growth of those under their care (2 Tim 2:25–26; 1 Pet 5:1–4). We cannot speak into someone's life until they see us model submission to the truth. Take time to listen carefully before you offer a response. A man with a pure heart and life doesn't speak rashly or harshly. Solomon hits the mark: "The heart of the righteous ponders how to answer, but the mouth of the wicked pours out evil things" (Prov 15:28). When you listen with a critic's spiritual best in your mind, you're able to see more objectively the real heart behind the criticism.

CLARIFICATION

Skilled listening also involves the understanding of terms and context. We should not neglect asking questions when greater clarity is needed. Be careful, however, that questions are not an attempt to divert attention from the central issue being raised, nor should they be asked in a challenging or inflammatory manner. Terminology is used differently by all of us, and we gain much ground when those involved can agree on the meaning of what is being said. A lot of criticism boils down to poor use of the English language or simple misunderstandings.

I recall one time when I was asked to review and approve a women's Bible study outline for an upcoming study. The main points were stated using metaphors, making it a bit difficult to understanding the biblical principles I was supposed to be approving. I wrote the teacher, mentioning that the outline was "metaphorical," and that I needed clarification on the biblical principle behind each metaphor. Suddenly, I found myself embroiled in a conflict I never intended. My request was transmitted through a third party (always risky), and when it reached the teacher, she thought I had accused her of using material that was too "metaphysical"! She was deeply hurt. I didn't even know what the word "metaphysical" meant, and I'm quite certain she didn't either. The conflict was unnecessary and rather hilarious, looking back on it. But the unfortunate misunderstanding brought no small amount of criticism against my leadership until I could help the women's ministry leaders see where the mistake occurred. Thankfully, the tension was short-lived, but simple misunderstandings don't always turn out as well. Asking good questions for clarification is essential to good listening. We must learn to respond to criticism with phrases such as "Help me understand … " or "Please be patient with me and tell me again what the issue is." Most people don't mind taking more time to explain themselves, and working toward fresh clarity is always safer than pushing for quick, but superficial, solutions.

GODLY RESPONSES

Good listeners respond in a way that makes it difficult for criticism to become further inflamed. Skilled listeners turn away wrath with a "soft answer" (Prov 15:1; 25:15). When you're criticized, even unjustly, you must listen without interrupting or forming snap-conclusions. Pouncing on the words and approach of others stirs up strife and causes people to become exasperated and discouraged. Indeed, offenses caused by making hasty judgments are the most difficult to erase. Proverbs 18:19 says, "A brother offended is more unyielding than a strong city, and quarreling is like the bars of a castle." Even if the criticism is fallacious, a good leader will not resort to *ad hominem* and blameshifting. Too often, leaders are rightly accused of being unapproachable because they attack everything about their critic—from the unbiblical process to the attitude in which the criticism comes. Inevitably, this promotes frustration, bitterness, and sinful assumptions about motives. We must be mature enough to see others through the eyes of Jesus Christ, who loved the unlovely and gave Himself for selfish sinners (Rom 5:6–10). The "process" by which a person levels criticism is never the primary issue, but rather the *content* of the negative evaluation! The question we ought to be asking when we hear criticism is "Lord, how can I learn from what this person is saying?"

Furthermore, leaders must develop the skill of bringing biblical, timely, and edifying speech to every issue, especially when answering criticism:

- We must learn to bring only God's wisdom to bear upon every issue and not human opinions (Prov 15:2; Eph 4:15; 2 Tim 3:16–17). Nothing is worse than adding human opinions to an already tense situation, yet we can sometimes respond to criticism with little or no thoughtful consideration of the Scriptures. In a dispute, the only opinion that matters is God's! We should be fearful of straying into the minefield of our own authority; we should be thinking to ourselves, "What does the Bible say about the issue?" and "What kind of response would most please the Lord?" When others see your passion for truth and willing submission to it, defenses come down and hearts soften. Conversely, if we imply the authority of our own opinions, others will get the message that we're not interested in even constructive critiques.

- We must learn to assess the best timing for a response to criticism (Prov 25:11; Col 4:6). When we become careless, we risk trampling the burdens and personal pain of others. Solomon's analogy of a happy songster in Proverbs 25:20 carelessly chiming away to someone in anguish paints the picture vividly: we might as well be removing the person's shirt in freezing weather! Good timing reflects that we know how human beings work through difficulty. It takes time for people to grow, both in their own sanctification and how they view the weaknesses of others. We already know that criticism often comes from poorly handled frustration and sinful assumptions. Good leaders must always remember the pace of their own sanctification, and acknowledge that others need time to change as well. We can't expect others to grow faster than we do. It's easy for us to assume that, as a general pattern, we respond to truth quickly and with little resistance. I may want to obey with a ready, willing heart, but I also know the truth about my sin better than anyone. Timely counsel blossoms from a relentless honesty about our own sanctification, causing us to be tenderly mindful of what others need in the moment. This isn't a call to passively allow others to continue in sin, but we do well to look for the best possible disposition in others before we tackle an issue. For instance, it is never helpful to abruptly correct someone's perspective when emotions are running high. As I have frequently told our congregation, "It sometimes takes a while for people's emotions to catch up with their theology." Nothing is solved by quickly pointing out the flaws of someone's complaining attitude before we've genuinely considered the accuracy of the complaint itself.

• Wise listeners always bring counsel that builds up the faith of another. When criticized, our speech should reflect our passion for the glory of Christ and the edification of His people. We are called to use speech that is "good for building up, as fits the occasion, that it may give grace to those who hear" (Eph 4:29). In the face of unfair criticism, how many of us are thinking about being a minister of grace to the person? Why is this so difficult? Because criticism forces us to look closely at potential weaknesses and limitations when we would rather stay on cruise control where we're comfortable. Consequently, we can quickly become like caged animals, looking for ways to hide weaknesses and discredit those who point them out. Our responses will always be sinful if we don't learn to pursue mutual edification at all costs. A complaint from others should alert us to the need for speech that is carefully seasoned and "gracious ... so that you may know how you ought to answer each person" (Col 4:6).

DEFENDING THE RIGHT CAUSE

Under some of the most relentless and malicious criticism ever endured by a leader, it is astounding that the apostle Paul never resorted to personal defensiveness or vengeful counter-attacks. In fact, when the Corinthian assembly finally repented for believing lies about Paul and running him out of town, they put Paul's main opponent under such severe discipline that Paul, rather than defend his own name and reputation, reminded them to forgive and comfort the man (2 Cor 2:6–7). Just when the temptation to vindicate himself might have been strongest, Paul defended the cause of truth. How could he be so strong on doctrine and yet so absorbing of personal attacks? Because Paul never took himself so seriously that he lost sight of his place in the kingdom work. He knew he was an expendable servant commissioned to do God's bidding; he was fully aware that ministry life, with its heartaches and disappointments, was a grace in his sanctification process. That's how he lived!

I'm frequently asked to explain the difficult balance between correcting false charges and resisting a personal defense. This is not a simple issue, but there are two principles that, as with Paul, help us respond well to personal attacks.

LEADERS SERVE THE PURPOSES OF GOD

We must not confuse what offends us and what offends God. Our personal pain and grief over unfair criticism must never overshadow the reality that all men do what they do in the presence of God (Heb 4:13)! Criticism of our leadership may be personally offensive and distasteful, especially when based upon falsities, but our allegiance is to the character and glory of the One who called us into service. Where God's name and character are belittled, we ought to be indignant. But when others attack our life and ministry, God remains the issue. He will bring everything to light at the proper time for the vindication of His glory and power (Matt 10:26; 1 Cor 4:5). We serve His purposes, which inevitably include attacks against His servants. People will "assail their leaders' character, criticize their decisions, speak evil behind their backs, and take advantage of their love"[3] but none of these things come close to how such behavior offends God. Taking personal offense at the attacks of others makes our reputation the issue and stores up personal "baggage" in our hearts, leading to bitter grudges. As Paul told the Corinthians in his first epistle, "What then is Apollos? What is Paul? Servants through whom you believed, as the Lord assigned to each. ... So neither he who plants nor he who waters is anything, but only God who gives the growth" (1 Cor 3:5, 7).

Defending our personal reputation by going on the attack directs attention toward us instead of the authority and glory of God. Criticism should be challenged, not when our reputation is maligned, but when God is. That's why Paul, in his second epistle to the Corinthians, defended his role as the *servant of God* in spite of harsh attacks against him personally. When he did defend his character, it was not with personal or vengeful counter-attacks against his critics, but rather by holding his character and ministry up to the scrutiny of God's standard. Reading the following defense of his ministry, we do not find even a hint of self-vindication:

> But as servants of God we commend ourselves in every way: by great endurance, in afflictions, hardships, calamities, beatings, imprisonments, riots, labors, sleepless nights, hunger; by purity, knowledge, patience, kindness, the Holy Spirit, genuine love, by truthful speech, and the power of God; with the weapons of righteousness for the right hand and for the left; through honor and dishonor, through slander and praise. We are treated as impostors, and yet are true; as unknown, and yet well known; as dying, and behold, we live; as punished, and yet not killed; as sorrowful, yet always rejoicing; as poor,

---

3   Ibid.

yet making many rich; as having nothing, yet possessing everything. (2 Cor 6:4–10)

Paul doesn't concern himself with the many persecutions, hardships, afflictions, or smear campaigns. He simply commends his life and ministry to others as a servant of the living God. Even though the entire second epistle to the Corinthian church was written as a defense of Paul's apostleship, he personally saw himself as of no personal account (2 Cor 12:12). Whatever the Lord willed, that's where Paul set his heart.

LEADERS LEARN THROUGH THE PURPOSES OF GOD

Criticism should be viewed as a tool for growth and change. Several temptations arise when we experience criticism: (1) We fear the loss of respect; (2) We look for reasons to challenge the data; (3) We search for flaws in the process; (4) We point out weakness in the other person; (5) We demand credit for our strengths; (6) We play the martyr, reeling under the unjust complaints of others. Yet, when we run away at the slightest hint of criticism we forfeit *the very means* by which the Lord wants to make us more effective and godly in our leadership. "Reproofs of discipline are the way of life" (Prov 6:23), Solomon said, and so we must use criticism to our spiritual advantage. We're frequently too afraid that others won't respect us if we acknowledge a shortfall, but the opposite is true. Self-defensive is a behavior that drains respectability from our leadership. On the danger of not "earning" the confidence of others, Borgman writes, "There is something very unbecoming about a man of God who is always defending himself. Whenever one makes an observation, raises a question or offers a rebuke, if walls of defense immediately go up, it erodes respect."[4]

---

4   Brian Borgman, *My Heart for Thy Cause* (Fearn, Ross-shire, Great Britain: Christian Focus, 2002), 99.

We need the sharpening that occurs when someone says "I dis-agree" or "I have a criticism" (cf. Prov 27:17). In fact, instead of yielding to the temptation of pride and fear of man, we ought to consider every criticism as a providential gift from the Lord to teach us some beneficial lessons:[5]

- Criticism drives us to prayer. A greater degree of depen-dency results when we're burdened over the criticism of others. We're compelled to take every matter before the Lord so that our hearts are guarded (Phil 4:6).

- Criticism drives us to the Scriptures. We are constrained to search the Word of God for clarity, wisdom, and under-standing (Ps 119:98–100; Prov 3:5–6; 2 Tim 3:16–17).

- Criticism refines our communication skills. We benefit from having to rearticulate what we believe in clearer terms and with a more careful disposition (Eph 4:29; Col 4:6).

- Criticism forces us to examine our hearts. Criticism causes us to look carefully at our attitudes and motives, and we are reminded of our own sinfulness (1 Cor 4:3–5; Gal 6:4-5).

- Criticism produces spiritual endurance. Being criticized may be painful, but God uses it to wean us from our own resources and make us stronger in His grace and strength (Jas 1:2–4; 2 Cor 12:7–10).

- Criticism provides unique opportunities to model godly humility. When others disagree, even sharply, we should be

---

5   I am indebted to Dr. Wayne Mack for some of these "benefits" which appear throughout his course materials on conflict resolution, particularly his premarital material (Wayne A. Mack, *Preparing for Marriage God's Way* [Tulsa, OK: Hensley Publishing, 1986]).

an example of humble submission to the Lord's sanctifying grace in our lives (Prov 9:8–9; 12:15).

- Criticism offers greater opportunity to give God glory. God is exalted and His glory magnified when His servants bear up graciously under harsh treatment (1 Pet 2:20; 3:15–17).

ACKNOWLEDGING WEAKNESS

Admitting faults to a critic is not pleasant. People often use our flaws as an excuse for not responding to our leadership. Though the Scriptures teach that we're all sheep in need of growth, that we all require the Lord's sanctifying grace, and that even a leader/shepherd should be allowed "progress" that everyone can observe (1 Tim 4:15), in the eyes of some, our credibility will irreparably suffer when we acknowledge a weakness. Hopefully, most will understand that we're just men, called of God, and trying to serve the needs of His flock while being an example.

When criticism comes, we must remember that our response *is* what we are modeling for others. The following principles help us eliminate defensiveness and pride:

- Search for any part of the criticism that is true and own it (Ps 51:4). If sin has occurred, seek forgiveness with humble gratitude for God's leading through that person (Prov 28:13; Jas 5:16).

- Make no demands on others to readily accept your admission. Disagreement between two parties is awkward enough, and the tension doesn't immediately wear off even though sin has been confessed and dealt with. People often need time for the grief of relational disharmony to dissipate. Once you've acknowledged a weakness, the tendency is to expect that person to quickly "shield" you from feelings of embarrassment and from the consequences of having failed. Let the Lord do His healing work, and trust that He always gives grace to the humble (Ps 138:6; Prov 3:34; Matt 3:12; 1 Pet 5:6–7).

- When a criticism has no merit, seek to understand how the person could have drawn his conclusions. Sometimes, people form wrong perceptions because of misunderstandings, false assumptions, misinformation, hearsay, etc. Learning how others have come to their ideas helps them see your concern for how your actions and words might have contributed to misconceptions. Following a criticism with "Your concern is unfounded, but I can clearly see how you could have perceived it that way" gives others the benefit of the doubt without assuming foolish ignorance or ill-motive on their part.

- If a complaint is leveled with sinful attitudes, forgive the offense quickly and lavishly, exercise self-control, and respond with carefully chosen words and attitudes (see under "Godly Responses" above).

ANSWERING FOOLS WISELY

There are criticisms that come from those who are satisfied with nothing less than destroying the work of God. If leaders try to silence every critic, chase down every rumor, and argue toe to toe with every ministry opponent, the work of service would never get done! I recall a time as a young shepherd in ministry when someone intent on starting a divisive movement against me began to strongly oppose my leadership and teaching. I asked a longtime veteran in the ministry what I should do. His counsel was clear, penetrating, and hugely encouraging! He said, "Well, you have the pulpit so you have the greatest platform for truth. Keep preaching powerful sermons. And remember, Nehemiah never came down off the wall to get embroiled in meetings with all of his critics. He

had a job to do for the Lord, and nothing deterred him from it."
I was immediately energized! Satan loves to throw every possible
distraction at us so that we forget to keep *the main thing the main
thing*. If criticism comes from the mouth of a fool, we are not to
descend to the level of petty arguments and non-essentials.

In Proverbs 26:4–5 we're given a strange set of back-to-back
principles: "Answer not a fool according to his folly, lest you be like
him yourself. Answer a fool according to his folly, lest he become
wise in his own eyes." What are we to make of these seemingly
contradictory admonitions? Notice that both texts involve the
words and deeds of a fool, and also that both texts guarantee a
result depending upon our response. According to verse 4, if we
answer a fool with similar words and deeds, we will adopt the
fool's character and behavior as our own. But if, as indicated in
verse 5, we answer the fool with words and deeds that challenge
his folly and pride, we become an agent of truth and wisdom in his
life. How does this apply to the criticism of a fool? It teaches us
that we should distinguish between critiques that originate from
foolishness and those that come from wisdom. A fool's criticism
will bear the following marks:

- dishonesty, tale-bearing, and slander (Prov 11:13; 3 John 10)
- separation from accountability (Prov 18:1)
- a quarrelsome spirit and strife-mongering (Prov 26:20; 6:19; 15:18)

The complaint of a fool deserves a response filled with strong
truth and a stern warning. It is a waste of time to get involved in
worthless disputes and petty arguments with those whose interest
is divisiveness. The Scriptures strictly warn leaders and shepherds
not to get enmeshed in "foolish controversies ... dissensions, and
quarrels ... for they are unprofitable and worthless. As for a person who stirs up division, after warning him once and then twice,
have nothing more to do with him, knowing that such a person is
warped and sinful; he is self-condemned" (Titus 3:9–11).

For spiritual leaders, criticism is a painful inevitability. It can come when we least expect it, and sometimes from the least likely sources. How we respond will be the difference between an excellent ministry and one that is plagued with strife. We need to hone our listening skills. We must resist taking personal offense when complaints are thrown at us. The kingdom work is God's business, and His glory should be our highest pursuit. When our reputation, our name, our achievements are paramount, we view criticism as a negative to be constantly avoided. But criticism is a sanctifying grace in the believer's life, and we can learn from the perceptions of others—both the accurate and mistaken.

Father, I am desperate for Your grace and strength in this area. When I'm criticized, I become immediately on edge and try to squirm out of its benefits. Challenge my heart with the truth that You're behind every complaint, doing a work in my life so that I might share in Your holiness more deeply. Show me the ways that my flaws hinder what You've called me to do. Ground me in Your truth so that I see clearly what to respond to and what to set aside. Amen.

9

NAVIGATING UNAVOIDABLE CONFLICT

The Church of Jesus Christ is the most glorious living organism ever conceived in the untraceable mind of God! She is the possession of God and the exquisite workmanship of His wise and holy character. She has been purchased with the precious blood of her Lord—the unrivaled head of the body! She is loved and adored by every saint, who by grace alone enjoys sweet entrance and fellowship. She is fiercely hated by Satan and his fallen hosts, and is continually under siege by the world, which cannot tolerate her powerful, living dynamic of sanctification. Her growth is divinely ordained, her endurance is superintended and assured, and her ultimate perseverance and final glory cannot be shaken! In fact, she will one day bring honor and glory to Jesus Christ *without stain or wrinkle*, in all holiness and majesty.

For now, however, the church is not yet purified, not yet clothed in final majesty, not yet the beautiful bride of heavenly splendor. We are in a daily battle with sin, locked in mortal combat and in a state of perpetual high alert. Striving together for the faith of the gospel, we pray for grace and look toward the blessed hope of the return of our Lord Jesus Christ! And the Holy Spirit has reconciled us to God through Christ. He has made us one with each other, and we are called to preserve our unity "in the bond of peace" (Eph 4:3). Sadly, though with one voice we worship our Prince of Peace, we often fail to make peace with one another. Factions in the church are all too common and very destructive.

In his first letter to the church in Corinth, Paul said, "God is faithful, by whom you were called into the fellowship of his Son, Jesus Christ our Lord. I appeal to you, brothers, by the name of our Lord Jesus Christ that all of you agree" (1 Cor 1:9–10). This is the clearest definition of unity in the church! We work for harmony in our understanding of truth and for unity in our obedience. Paul went on to say that we should not allow divisions to fester, but we should "be united in the same mind and the same judgment" (1 Cor 1:10). He told the Philippian church, "[I want you to] complete my joy by being of the same mind" (Phil 2:2). It's a complete, riveting, pastoral joy when the flock is "of the same mind, having the same love, being in full accord and of one mind" (Phil 2:2). What is the key ingredient for such oneness of doctrine and devotion? It is simple: we are to be humble like the Lord Jesus.

If we can prevent conflicts, then we must work to prevent them. We ought not to accept that there will always be the same necessary battles. Some are necessary, but some are unnecessary. And if we cannot prevent them, then we must resolve them biblically, pursuing every possible means of peace. Romans 12:18 says, "If possible, so far as it depends on you, live peaceably with all." We cannot control what others do, but we have a responsibility to resolve the tensions that arise in church ministry and leadership. And we are to do so in a way that honors Christ.

IT BEGINS WITH THE SHEPHERD

As disheartening as conflict is among sheep, *far more devastating are sinful divisions* within the leadership. God's people are called to agree with one another, and the shepherds of the church are called to lead the way. But often it is a leader's immature and sinful approach to conflict that turns a spark into a forest fire.

Pastors sometimes take criticism personally and become defensive. The church becomes weak when leaders bring more tension and personal offenses to the conflict. Paul's young disciple, Timothy, was warned about the tendency in leaders to become quarrelsome (2 Tim 2:24) when things don't go their way. But if a pastor can restrain his defensiveness and see conflict as a sanctifying grace in his life, he will be able to minister greatly to those hurt by a divided fellowship. In fact, leaders without grudges are especially useful in shepherding those who have caused division in the first place.

This is precisely how Paul was able to diffuse the factions in Corinth and become a true instrument of grace, even to the man who, out of bitterness against Paul, originally caused the dissension. In 2 Corinthians 2:4 Paul says, "I wrote to you out of much affliction and anguish of heart and with many tears, not to cause you pain but to let you know the abundant love that I have for you." The church at Corinth had recently come out of a massive conflict. Paul had planted the church and had spent considerable time there teaching, shepherding, and establishing leaders before he left. It wasn't long before those who opposed his ministry infiltrated the congregation, slandering Paul and undermining his pastoral influence. By the time he returned to strengthen the ministry, the church had already been swayed. Three months into his visit they put him out of the church. This was a devastating faction that could potentially undo Paul's gospel effort in other churches under the shadow of the Corinthian ministry.

Despite the slander against Paul's reputation, he took steps to shepherd the leaders in the essentials of striving for peace. He kept his own heart from taking personal offense while defending the integrity of his pastoral life among them. And when the church—and particularly the ringleader of the faction—repented, Paul helped prevent the church's overreaction against all those who caused the split: "Now if anyone has caused pain, he has caused it not to me, but in some measure—not to put it too severely—to all of you. For such a one, this punishment by the majority is enough" (2 Cor 2:5–6). The church discipline process had broken hearts and produced a godly sorrow. It was crucial at that point to heal relationships and prevent further trauma caused by retaliating against the leader or leaders who were responsible. If they were truly repentant, Paul did not want a recently restored brother to be "overwhelmed by excessive sorrow" (v. 7).

We do well to learn from the heart of Paul when shepherding our congregations through the pain of a church split. Our sole focus should be the honor of Christ in His church. Therefore, it is crucial that leaders lay aside all personal offenses. When pastors model self-restraint, absorbing the pain of personal offenses and pointing others to the worthiness of Jesus Christ, unity flourishes. Many times a conflict simply will not die a natural death because church leaders give it life support by punishing those who have hurt them. When pastors return insult for insult the sheep are prone to follow. Paul was a model of putting Christ's reputation and gospel ministry first, no matter how much criticism he personally endured. He strongly urged the Corinthians to honor the Lord with a peacemaking heart. Even though Paul had been severely abused by a factious leader and all those influenced by the slander against his ministry, his deepest concern was not his own reputation but that of his Lord and Savior. Such pastoral humility was the spiritual force behind the words: "So I beg you to reaffirm your love for him. For this is why I wrote, that I might test you and know whether you are obedient in everything" (vv. 8–9).

For many years I served under a nationally and internationally recognized pastor whose decades of tireless preaching and shepherding are to this day frequently misrepresented, and his motives often judged and scorned. Year after year I watched up close and in awe as this faithful man of God forgave offenses, kept no record of wrongs, and sought to bless his adversaries. This was the key to the steadiness of his ministry. He carried no sack of personal offenses over his shoulder, daring someone to give him a reason to dump its contents. Such kindness toward opponents remains one of the most profound ministry training grounds I was

ever privileged to enjoy. I learned the high priority of a clean conscience, and I learned to love mercy, which triumphs over judgment (Mic 6:8; Jas 2:13). Conflicts, together with their destructive fallout, are minimized greatly when pastors guard their hearts
against the very sins they counsel others to flee.

But conflict will be unavoidable. You can try to carry out a life
of ministry without dissension, a church split, or serious disunity
among leaders, but inevitably wherever sinners gather to have gospel influence there will be conflict. The soil out of which conflict
grows is filled with different seedbeds of discord. Many of these
seedbeds are beyond our control and make conflict inevitable
because of the gospel's collision with evil. There are conflicts we
can and must avoid (the sinful kind), but there are also those divisions which have nothing to do with our sin against others. These
we must face so that we are spiritually refined and so that the
faithful are clearly distinguished from the apostate (1 Cor 11:19).
The unavoidable kind of conflict rises from two different seedbeds: Satanic assault and human differences.

SATANIC ASSAULT

Satan wants us to "bite and devour one another" (Gal 5:15), and
he'll use every evil nutrient at his disposal to nourish a forest of
factions. First, he schemes to introduce deceit, disunity, and a lack
of integrity in the church. At the birth of the church, Acts 5:3
describes how Satan filled the heart of Ananias and Sapphira to
lie to the Holy Spirit and deceive God's people. 2 Corinthians
11:14–15 warns that Satan comes to devour the church by pre-
senting his servants as innocent, but they are deceitful. They present themselves as "angels of light." Peter tells us, "Your adversary
the devil prowls around like a roaring lion, seeking someone to
devour" (1 Pet 5:8).

Second, he promotes the spirit of antichrist all around God's
people in order to deceive them. As Ephesians 2:2 teaches, Satan is
behind it all: "You once walked, following the course of this world,

following the prince of the power of the air, the spirit that is now at work in the sons of disobedience." That spirit is always actively assaulting the church and frequently infiltrates the leadership. Third, false leaders use their influence to divide the church. In Acts 20:29–30 Paul tells the elders of the church in Ephesus, "I know that after my departure fierce wolves will come in among you, not sparing the flock; and from among your own selves will arise men speaking twisted things, to draw away the disciples after them."

Fourth, the hatred of the world brings distress upon the church. In John 15:18–19 Jesus told His disciples that the world's hatred would come at them because He chose them out of the world. The world hated Christ first, and that is why the world hates Christ's people. In Acts 14:22, Paul and Barnabas were "strengthening the souls of the disciples, encouraging them to continue in the faith, and [they were] saying that through many tribulations we must enter the kingdom of God." Many tribulations! Has anyone ever made that passage their life verse? Not likely. Yet in 2 Timothy 3:12 Paul writes, "Indeed, all who desire to live a godly life in Christ Jesus will be persecuted."

HUMAN DIFFERENCES

Some conflict is rooted in common differences among the leaders of the church. Our differences may seem rather benign, yet they affect the way we view ministry and the decisions we make in serving the church. God has made us diverse. That is the wonderful adventure of ministry. I call it "The Master's Mix." We come from diverse backgrounds, we look at life through different lenses, we express strong emotional attachment to some aspects of ministry and show very little concern about other aspects. God calls elders to the task and He gifts them accordingly. But He also gives us very different "wiring," which is essentially the natural lens through which ministry decisions are evaluated. Elders will serve the church very well if each of them identifies, to whatever degree, their particular natural tendencies. I'm convinced that a lot of conflict at the leadership level could be greatly reduced if pastors and leaders simply knew their idiosyncrasies, enjoyed the peculiarities of others, and were humble enough to defer to one another in love.

MINISTRY IMMATURITIES

Leadership teams are funny things. I have watched them for a long time and have noticed areas of common diversity from which conflicts can arise. The first area of diversity is *ministry immaturities*. Pastors need to grow spiritually, and until we mature in particular areas, our immature thought processes can spark conflict. For example, leaders might have only a surface understanding of certain key doctrines. The bottom line is that some shepherds do not know their Bibles well enough. Conflict arises from this immaturity when we are asked questions about Scripture and theology which we have not thought through very well. Or we answer a biblical question with a common sense principle from the business world rather than principles from Scripture. Biblical illiteracy or theological ignorance at the elder level causes a lack of clarity in decision making. We find it hard to separate principles from preferences. We invoke God's authority in areas where His Word says little or nothing. We may even hold tenaciously to a doctrine we have never studied in depth and therefore cannot personally defend. Conflicts at the leadership level are often traced back to a lack of maturity in the clarity of Scripture as it applies to church life.

Ministry immaturities also derive from the lack of practiced spiritual disciplines. We expect younger leaders to struggle in the cultivation of spiritual disciplines—to take seriously their leadership role. But sometimes it is the more seasoned veterans who have never exercised their spiritual muscles in key areas of their walk with Christ. In all other ways they may be godly and willing to serve, yet their biblical discernment and insight are lacking. Many leadership decisions present multiple challenges and require nuanced applications of Scripture. A pastor who lacks spiritual discipline will often be unaware of how to wisely apply truth to delicate situations. Wisdom in the skilled application of Scripture comes by disciplined practice (Heb 5:14). Without it, leaders will bring much immature thinking into the process, which adds frustration and puts leaders at odds.

Another ministry immaturity is the lack of courage. Men who lack courage have not had enough ministry experience to refine their faith and build spiritual endurance (Jas 1:2–4). In a word, they don't trust the Lord as robustly as they ought when trouble comes. Faith needs to be tested, and theirs is still young and unproven. Courage comes from seeing the Lord's faithfulness through the dark valleys of ministry. It comes from having to believe God when all circumstances are set against us. Spiritual courage is forged in the fires of standing alone for Christ and being upheld "in the strength of His might" (Eph 6:10). And great courage comes from seeing the ministry through the eyes of the Great Shepherd, who, unlike hirelings, will not flee but lays down His life for His sheep (John 10:12–15). Conflict occurs when leadership solidarity is weakened by leaders who walk away from their post due to the cost being too great for them. They have to gain experience trusting the Lord through the hardships of ministry.

Ministry immaturities also include the lack of relational skills. Balanced leadership requires that we develop the ability to interact graciously and carefully in multiple contexts with people of all backgrounds. Yet some pastors never seem to learn the joy and value of understanding the diversity within the body of Christ. They chafe at having to think about adjusting to the concerns and preferences of others. In fact, many leaders create conflict because they've never honed the skill of learning other people's strengths and weaknesses so as to be a complement to a group effort. They behave as though others should conform to their way of thinking and how they solve problems. Leadership teams, however, are to preserve unity within a diversity. An elder board is a team. It is a plurality of men called by God to serve the church. They are different, yet they serve the same Lord and follow the same instruction manual—Scripture.

UNIQUE PERSONALITIES

The second area of common diversity from which conflict can arise is even more peculiar. We could call it *unique personality traits* or simply the way God "wired" us. A leadership team will often be a collection of such diverse personalities that the potential for conflict is high. For instance, there are pessimists and optimists. Pessimists tend to think that optimists are oblivious to reality, while optimists think pessimists are whiners and complainers. Of course, each thinks they represent greater balance when it comes to tough decisions. The pessimist thinks he's a realist and therefore assumes he's wiser in decision making, but the optimist thinks his more hopeful outlook reflects great faith, and therefore he has the greater discernment.

Another personality clash occurs between the artistic type of leader and the linear-minded engineer of the group. Artistic people tend to assume that engineer types will turn shepherding into a math equation and calculate the sheep into sanctification, while engineer types see artists as more or less older hippies who often run on emotion. Add to the tumultuous mix the compassionate and the hardline leader. The compassionate person is merciful, and they view hardliners as mostly unloving. But hardliners assume that merciful people are sentimental and relatively weak. Yet another peculiar category of opposites is the frugal person and the risk-taker. The frugal tend to see risk-takers as irresponsible and poor stewards of God's resources. Frugal leaders like to run the church finances the way they do at home, according to their personal spending habits. But risk-takers see frugal people as stingy and faithless. Discussions over significant financial decisions within the church often end in a stalemate:

"Brother, you need to have some faith."

"Yes, but you just wanted to increase the budget thirty percent. That's not faith, that's crazy."

More often than not, conflict at this level is rooted in merely how God has "wired" us. It may not result in the worst kinds of sin, but it creates huge tension on a leadership team.

There are also the opposing groups I like to call the fighters and the flee-ers. The fighters tend to spoil for a good argument. They're always at the ready, leaning up to the table, and can't wait till someone lights the fuse. But the flee-ers, it seems, do not stay and fight for anything. Fighters see the flee-er as compromising, yet it may just be different wiring. Sometimes the flee-er sees himself as a peacemaker and the fighter never seems to be making peace, so they're perceived as less spiritual—again, creating tension. The flee-er sees the fighter as unnecessarily offensive and the fighter sees himself as a ministry gatekeeper.

Two final categories: problem solvers and ostriches. The problem solver is the impatient fixer. He has to get it resolved and loathes any kind of lingering tension. This is typically the same kind of leader who talks until two in the morning to get his wife to resolve an issue. He has to have it fixed or else he can't function the next day. But the ostrich is the negligent ignorer. For fear of tension he puts his head in the ground hoping the problem will go away. The ostrich thinks that he's being patient and sees the fixer as impatient, and the fixer sees the ostrich as running from trouble, not willing to get his hands dirty.

The tensions that come from differing ways God has "wired" us do not have to become serious factions. How often have leaders allowed tensions to arc, taking offense and assuming motives, yet the cause is simply a case of crossed wiring? When we begin to understand how God has made us and our corresponding tendencies, we are better equipped to work in harmony with those of different—even quite opposite—perspectives. Adding different levels of ministry maturity to the struggle only increases the potential for conflict. One leader lacks courage and another runs to the battle. One elder is more practiced in the spiritual disciplines while another is slowly learning them. There are leaders with polished relational skills—perhaps natural to his personality—but another leader is more uncomfortable in group settings. These are not willful patterns of weakness brought on by sinful neglect. Nevertheless, they are significant differences which often spark tensions. If not understood as to their source, these conflicts can cause unnecessary disunity, which weakens a leadership team and inevitably hurts God's people.

VARYING HISTORIES

One final category of common diversity: *varying histories*. Our personal history—our background—will shape the way we function as leaders. Most of us assume this is the case and imagine we can work together with others without majoring on minor differences. But often we do not realize how strongly we feel about an area of ministry until the issue presents itself. For instance, when deciding whether to borrow money for an expansion of facilities, a typically low-key elder may express strong opposition to the church taking on debt. His own personal history of handling money has contributed to the level of passion behind his viewpoint. As others express different perspectives, the elder, caught off guard in the intensity of his views, digs in his proverbial heels. It is crucial at such times for men to help each other discover how our personal history may have a negative effect on our ability to lead with balance.

What is behind these moments of sudden tension and rising passion within us? What makes an otherwise balanced leader suddenly immovable over what appear to be personal issues? Well, sometimes the cause is our former training. Each leader brings to the team a history of experiences. We listen to the voices of previous mentors whom we highly respect. When fellow leaders push against the views of our former teachers, we become very passionate, not realizing that our intensity is being fueled by our desire to ardently defend those who trained us. In fact, we may have never studied the issue at hand, but our mentors and former training are held in such high esteem that we will even defend error unawares.

Another area of our varying histories has to do with church experience. Were we exposed to spiritually healthy ministries? Has church life been one massive and hurtful conflict after another? I recall one pastor saying that his current leadership structure is a reaction to how many times he had "been burned" by those he had previously trusted. The way we view church polity and body life is heavily influenced by our experiences in previous ministries. Perhaps you witnessed the increasing pride of a formerly humble leader, which has made you suspicious of gifted pastors and any level of ministry success. Or while serving in your previous church you experienced serious "burnout," which causes you to hold back from meeting needs while constantly warning fellow leaders of the dangers. Understanding our reactions to previous difficulties in ministry greatly reduces the potential for serious conflict within a leadership team. We need to be aware of unchecked fears that are affecting our ability to make decisions objectively.

We must also consider how we have been influenced by the leadership structure of previous ministries. Was it an elder-led church? Did that structure seem to flourish? Was it a ministry committed to a congregational rule polity? What kind of tensions did that structure create? Were all decisions voted on by everyone? Was unanimity required, or merely a majority? Whatever your church background, you bring that experience—that leadership grid—with you as you serve your current ministry. And make no mistake, changes in your personal convictions about leadership structure and church polity tend to come slowly. I'm not suggesting, however, that our diverse backgrounds are chiseled in stone so that we are typecast in these traits. On the contrary, when we understand the way our personal ministry background shapes the way we make decisions and lead others, we are able to identify any biases we might have in a particularly challenging situation.

As leaders learn one another, we are able to laugh together at these tendencies, and encourage one another toward greater balance. Instead of assuming we are objective and our fellow leaders need correction, we must be willing to face our tendencies, learn their root causes, and understand how we are perceived by others in our leadership strengths and limitations. In order to truly know ourselves and our leadership tendencies, it requires more than mere self-examination. We learn much from how others perceive us as well. Are we willing to say to a team of fellow servants, *"I'm here to be shaped. I'm here to learn my tendencies and their root causes. I want to be the most useful vessel in the service of Christ that I can be"?* We may not be able to avoid the conflict that comes from these rather benign areas of diversity, but we can prevent them from becoming unnecessary schisms if we handle them with humility, careful understanding, and Christlike love.

> *Lord, I come before You and confess my neediness in this great privilege to lead Your people. I'm a flawed man called to imitate You and to call others to imitate me as I imitate You. I rejoice in how You have fashioned me. Yet I realize that such handiwork is also heavily influenced by the circumstances of life and my responses to them. My leadership of Your sheep reflects these nuances. May I never see myself as a perfect balance. May I lead with a sensitivity to the tendencies I bring to the group of men You have raised up to lead this flock. I want to be strong in the grace that is in Christ. I need wisdom and insight to navigate these challenging areas. I trust Your love and Your surgeon's hand to do Your work in me for the protection of the flock and for the glory of Your name. Amen.*

10

PREVENTING AND RESOLVING CONFLICT

S everal years ago our church went through a season of conflict which was potentially volatile and ministry-splitting. A number of World War II veterans in the church—including a senior elder—were concerned that a recent refurbishment of the auditorium had resulted in the removal of the American flag. Our nation's colors had been flown somewhat prominently since the church's beginning in the 1920s. For the senior saints of the ministry, displaying an American flag in the church wasn't a political statement, but a matter of honor and respect. American lives had been sacrificed so that citizens of this great country could worship freely according to our beliefs. Yet, what for one generation was a statement of gratitude to fallen comrades became for a younger generation a matter of potentially confusing politics with gospel ministry. *"The church is not a political institution; the pulpit is not a platform for the cultural agenda,"* the younger generation declared. Older saints simply could not understand such sentiment. They had never imagined that the church's mission—the gospel of Christ—could potentially be supplanted by a political agenda merely through the respectful display of an American flag. The disagreement had the potential to become seriously divisive, and our leadership team would need to carefully consider how to proceed.

At a Wednesday evening body life meeting, I asked the congregation to give the leadership three months to study the issue from a biblical perspective and formally present the results. Since this occurred early on in my ministry alongside my elders, this would give us the opportunity to cultivate our relationships as elders as well as look to the Scriptures together and be refined in our discernment. At the time, our team of men varied in ages, but about half of them were seniors and the other half were much younger and less experienced in life and ministry. It would be a challenge to separate preferences from biblical mandates, but we were determined to strive for unity. Once conflict had become unavoidable, we needed wisdom principles to work our way through it in a way that would honor the Lord. The principles had to be grounded in Scripture, and then, of course, they could be wisely applied well beyond the current conflict. As we studied the issue, the following leadership principles became very helpful to us in the process.

PRAY FOR ONE ANOTHER

Never underestimate the need to *pray* for and *encourage* one another. It seems a rather obvious principle, yet we often rush to resolve conflicts without first entering the throne room of grace together so that our hearts are properly aligned with the God of peace. Paul admonishes us to "let the peace of Christ rule in [our] hearts" (Col 3:15), which is to say that the peace we enjoy with God should govern how we respond in conflicts with one another. Christ reconciled us to God. It is His peaceable disposition toward us that makes peace with others possible. In other words, the "peace of Christ" should be the umpire of all our disputes. Praying over these truths beforehand calibrates our attitudes. This is, no doubt, why Paul often referred to his running and rather lengthy list of ministry burdens over which he prayed continuously. We tend to bypass this critical first step because our daily routine involves problem solving almost hourly. Taking time to pray over a conflict, however, cultivates humility and softens our hearts toward one another. When we pray, our sinful desires cannot make progress, but are stopped in their tracks.

CONFRONT ONE ANOTHER IN LOVE

Resolving conflict requires that all sin be confronted, confessed, forsaken, and forgiven. Seeking wisdom together demands that "the goal of our instruction is love from a pure heart and a good conscience and a sincere faith (1 Tim 1:5, NASB). We will never reach unity by ignoring sinful attitudes and actions. Nor can we think biblically with a bludgeoned conscience (1 Tim 1:6). Tension at the leadership level is always uncomfortable, and some leaders imagine that they can think clearly through body life challenges without first dealing with sinful offenses. This is a serious miscalculation. Church leaders must be clean vessels, "sanctified, useful to the Master, prepared for every good work" (2 Tim 2:21). Uncomfortable or not, we must be willing to gently confront one another in love so that all sin is righted and relationships restored. It's no wonder that many leadership teams can't seem to make wise decisions for the church: so often they have tried to conduct ministry while unresolved sin boils below the surface, looking for a place to erupt. We serve the people of God best when, as one of my mentors used to say, "we place ourselves in the place of God's maximum blessing."[1] It means that we must, "so far as it depends on [us], live peaceably with all" (Rom 12:18).

---

[1]   This expression has been embedded into my heart and mind down through the years. Dr. John MacArthur, alongside whom I labored for ten years, repeated these words to me many times in the challenges of ministry. It has served to remind me that all effective ministry is the work of the Spirit of God, and that I am most able to be a blessing to the flock when I've kept a clean conscience and lived a pure life.

HUMBLY ACKNOWLEDGE YOUR FLAWS

When you are the one on the other end of a confrontation, that is when humility is needed most. The Lord looks to those who are "humble and contrite in spirit and trembles" at His Word (Isa 66:2). Pride kills the wisdom needed to lead the church. There is no denying that all leaders bring some level of pride and arrogance to our ministries labors. The conscientious shepherd may strive for humility and not see a prideful blind spot until it is pointed out, but all leaders must face pride in our hearts in all its various forms. Preventing and resolving sinful conflicts in the church will be impossible if leaders refuse to resolve sin in their own hearts. When our sin is noted, we should pray for humility, seek to understand the cause of our error, ask for forgiveness from the offended, thank the Lord and that person for loving you enough to confront the sin, and enlist the prayers of fellow leaders as a safeguard against your weaknesses. Also, resist the temptation to draw inward and away from the men in the needs of the ministry. A strong leadership team is a merciful and gracious one. Faithfully engage one another, encourage and help one another, and honor Christ together for the strength He provides in the tensions and conflicts of church life.

EMBRACE TRIBULATIONS

Tribulation does a mighty work in your life. The discipline of the Lord that comes through such tribulations is intended to increase our virtue (Heb 12:4–13). Church leaders must model steadfastness during the trials of life and ministry. Perhaps you've never thought of a text such as James 1:2–4 as applicable to the struggles of church leadership. We tend to think about trials as circumstances that we face personally rather than tests facing the leaders of the church. It is crucial, however, that we view the difficulties of ministry life in the same way we view other trials and tribulations. We must lead by cultivating a James 1:2–4 perspective. God tests the leadership of a church with the same purpose for which He sends trials into our personal lives. He uses leadership challenges to build endurance, which leads to settled rest, greater holiness, and more discernment. Without this perspective we default to fleshly responses of sinful fear, self-will, and reliance on human wisdom. We must model what it means to trust the Lord in the difficulties of life—and conflict in the church is where this is manifested vividly.

HUMBLE LEADERS DON'T RUN FROM CONFLICT

The church body is encouraged and stabilized when they see leaders submitting to trials. Trials wean us from selfish tendencies, but running from conflict—as the hireling of John 10:12–13—brings eventual discouragement because problems never get addressed. A leadership team may have two or three men who never want to engage, letting others do the heavy lifting in a conflict. They may believe they are helping, but if such neglect continues, their spiritual vitality and biblical clarity will go from bad to worse. Soon they will be unable to apply the Scriptures with competence. Embracing trials as a grace from the Lord to strengthen and sharpen us is absolutely essential for a healthy leadership team and ministry. Spiritual muscles are exercised and character is further refined.

HUMBLE LEADERS DON'T SPOIL FOR CONFLICT

On the other hand, while we must not run from conflict, we should never take pleasure in a ministry firefight. Mature leaders have a healthy dislike for tension, conflict, and negative influences in the work of the church. I won't back down where the care of the sheep is concerned, yet there is always a sense of grief that comes with conflict. Resolving tension almost always takes more time than anticipated, and meetings are usually filled with difficult and very personal confrontation, all requiring very delicate speech. Getting into meetings like this with aggressive personalities is not fun. It is what godly leaders dread most. If one of your men seems to enjoy intramural debates and tension-filled interactions, he will likely create more conflict than he diffuses. We must be humble, never glorying in disagreements and the tension they produce, but always doing everything we can to prevent further conflict (2 Tim 2:24).

SEPARATE PERSONAL PREFERENCES FROM BIBLICAL PRINCIPLES

In a conflict, it is crucial that we determine whether the trouble stems from a personal preference or a biblical principle. As mentioned earlier, people were very passionate about the American flag being displayed in the auditorium. Notably, the flag itself is of greater importance to me, having served for a time in the U. S. military. I'm a veteran, and as much as I see the paganism growing in this country and know the inevitability of what God says in Romans 1, I am still thankful to have served our country so that we can continue enjoying our religious freedoms. Our senior elder, who is with the Lord now, lost family members in World War II, and he himself fought on the frontlines in Italy. My military service was much later, during peacetime. Consequently, these older, battle-seasoned men were giants in my mind. I was sympathetic to those whose brothers were killed on the beaches of Normandy.

At the same time, I also resonated with the younger generation in our church who were asking, *"Is our church about gospel ministry or politics?"* Sometimes it is very difficult to draw a clear line between a biblical principle and a preference because the issues may be rooted in biblical principles generally and yet our applications are more preferential. The flag dilemma in our church was nuanced in that way. Some thought that if God gave us religious freedoms worth fighting for, then to remove our nation's flag from the auditorium would be disrespectful of our ancestors' sacrifices. To war veterans, the flag for which blood was spilled represents the reason we are able to freely proclaim the gospel from our pulpits. In their minds, removing the flag didn't make sense. Meanwhile the younger generation sees the fallout of the church's attempt to win culture wars—to use political clout in a fight to maintain the freedoms we now find being threatened. In their minds, the gospel could be cheapened further by confusing the purpose of the church with culture wars and politics.

Our leadership team could identify with the strongly held views on both sides. In these very nuanced applications of the truth, leaders must help the sheep to separate clear biblical mandates from personal preferences. Despite the strong emotions often tied to our preferences, they remain mere preferences and should not be elevated to a level equal with Scriptural commands. Yet while the flag issue may have boiled down to strongly held preferences, we had to determine if deference could be shown to others in this case in order that love could prevail. In the end, we opted to ask the congregation to defer to the preference of our senior saints and resident veterans out of love for all that they held dear. Though not in any prominent place, we allowed the flag to remain in the auditorium for a few more years as it had been for decades. We also, however, decided to warn the senior believers that if the presence of the American flag were to ever cause anyone confusion as to the purpose of the church it would be immediately removed. Had our elders been unable to separate biblical principles from personal preferences, an already tension-filled issue could have caused a significant division in the church.

LETTING LOVE PREVAIL

If an issue involves personal preferences or matters of conscience, we must learn to defer to one another in love. In Romans 14:1–23 Paul teaches that each of us is to let love prevail in preferential issues. We stand or fall under the Lordship of Christ, and we have the promise from Him that He "is able to make [us] stand" (Rom

14:4). It is never right to judge others according to our preferences (Rom 14:10–13), as if what we prefer carries the authority of a biblical command. Church conflicts often escalate because leaders have not helped the sheep clearly distinguish between something God mandates and something that merely bothers our conscience personally. We may find ourselves strongly defending an issue as though God were concerned, yet Scripture says nothing at all about the matter. On the other hand, we may mistake a biblical mandate for a personal preference and be guilty of disobeying God in ignorance. Conflicts and sinful factions are diffused when principles and preferences are kept distinct.

SPIRIT-LED UNANIMITY ON EXPLICIT DOCTRINE AND MINISTRY PRINCIPLES

Where explicit doctrine and biblical principles are concerned, we should strive for complete unanimity as a leadership team. If full agreement has not yet been reached, we have the privilege of studying God's Word until the Spirit aligns our understanding. Biblical principles are immovable. How we conduct ministry in the life of the church should be clearly grounded in the mandates of Scripture. We should expect to "attain to the unity of the faith" (Eph 4:13) when dealing with doctrine and its practical outworking. Without clear lines between biblical commands and matters of preference, leadership decisions will descend into battles over strong opinions. Conflict cannot be resolved when we invoke God's authority where He does not speak, nor can we argue using mere opinions where He has spoken clearly.

Where personal preferences are at stake, we have an opportunity to lovingly defer to one another. Humility, grace, and personal sacrifice are death blows to conflict in the church. Unity and harmony are achieved when there is a willingness to "count others more significant than yourselves" (Phil 2:3), and to "outdo one another in showing honor" (Rom 12:10). The reason so many drastic shifts and changes were muscled into the church through the pragmatic movement is the immaturity and aggressiveness of younger saints. Had they sought unanimity on explicit doctrine and ministry principles, and then majored on humility and deference on all preferences, we might not have seen so much discord in the last few decades over how to proclaim the gospel to the culture.

Deferring Well

But when deferring, how do we genuinely set aside strong preferences and not grow bitter? First, we must remember what it means to defer. Showing deference simply means:

1. We are convinced that the matter at hand is one of personal preference rather than clear biblical principles.

2. We are not bound in our conscience to hold one opinion over another.

3. We are willing to defer to the collective wisdom and/or majority opinion of other leaders.

4. We trust that God is providentially working out His purposes as leaders weigh the options before them.

5. We are committed to being grateful for the harmony nurtured through deference.

6. We are committed to supporting the united decision of the leadership when called to give an answer to the congregation.

Second, deference to other leaders should be offered in a spirit of grateful stewardship. The ministry—and its many leadership dilemmas over matters of preference—is a privilege and a gift of grace. We are servants who offer our lives as a living sacrifice to the people of God. It is selfish therefore to put a stranglehold on other leaders or on ministry progress over mere preferences. We may hold to our opinions quite passionately, but where the

Bible does not speak, we must preserve the unity of the Spirit, deferring with a thankful heart for being counted worthy to serve God's people. We must not allow deference to turn to discouragement and fear. Once our hearts begin to nurture a dislike for the preferential views of others and the decisions they influence, resentment will soon follow.

Third, if you find that your conscience is greatly troubled by the preferences of other leaders, it is prudent to study Romans 14 as a safeguard against sinfully judging those whose conscience lands differently. And where a number of leadership decisions continue to raise tensions within your conscience, you should seriously consider stepping away from the burden of overseeing the church. There is no shame in leaving the mantle of oversight to those better able to navigate the tension of preferential nuances while you flourish in other fitting areas of service. The Lord desires that we bloom where He plants us in His vineyard (1 Cor 12:11, 18, 24–25). And let's be candid: it may take some leaders months or even years of internal turmoil before admitting their struggle. We may defer knowing that it will prevent a firestorm on the outside, yet we're unable to calm the tempest within. Such realizations should cause us to seek trusted and wise fellow leaders in order to revisit decisions in question. We must acknowledge that our attempt to defer has simply not matured past mere resignation. After further clarification, an honest assessment of our hearts, and much prayer, we should either humbly defer with a clear conscience or joyfully step away from that particular level of leadership.

Finally, deferring in matters of preference requires that we communicate leadership decisions in a way that prevents divisions among the sheep. The destructive fire of sinful conflict in churches is often traced back to elder-arson. Close personal relationships that develop among certain sheep and their shepherds are natural and edifying. However, it is difficult to remain objective in such dynamics, especially when the strong opinions of our dearest friends align so closely with ours. We sometimes defer among the elders behind closed doors to the strengthening of our bond of peace, only to weaken that bond in conversation with close ministry partners among the sheep. What we communicate may seem harmless—*"Well, I thought the decision was unwise, but I was overruled and so I deferred"*—but it's often the spark that burns down a forest of gospel influence. Sheep thrive on unity within the flock. Division at the leadership level confuses the flock and leaves them vulnerable to Satan's devices.

It is also crucial that leaders wisely encourage their spouse to humbly "obey [their] leaders and submit to them," knowing that God has called men to serve as leaders in the church who will "give an account" for decisions in ministry (Heb 13:17; cf. 1 Tim 2:12). Opinions shared with a spouse within the walls of a leader's home are appropriately insulated and hemmed in by close-range shepherding in marriage. When a leader's wife finds herself strongly opposed to elder decisions, she may be tempted to express her disapproval to close friends. This is not helpful at best, and a danger to the unity of the Spirit at worst. When we talk of private leadership matters to someone not directly involved, we place a massive burden on that person. From then on they will be accountable for how that information affects others and the ministry. Do they need to know what they were told? Are they spiritually mature enough to bear the burden of knowing such details? Will this become an occasion for the eventual spread of gossip and slander?

We're warned in Scripture about how our hearts are prone to love receiving information so that we feel more significant than others—empowered by knowing juicy details while others remain in the dark. Proverbs 18:8 bluntly says, "The words of a whisperer are like delicious morsels; they go down into the inner parts of the body." As the adage goes, information is power. The "inside scoop" of ministry carries with it a tremendous responsibility to guard sensitive information. A leader's wife may not be mature enough to handle hearing about decisions and the surrounding tensions. Deferring well means carefully shepherding all those within your direct sphere of influence. Those brought into the information loop—especially a spouse—must follow your example in deferring with joy to the decisions made for the direction of the ministry.

MAINTAIN A BROADER PERSPECTIVE

The next significant principle to remember in the middle of a conflict is to maintain a broader perspective on the progress of the gospel. What do I mean? Well, in a conflict we tend to get myopic. Like being six inches from a wall mural, seeing only the smallest segment of the artwork, the minutiae of a conflict can begin to narrow our view of things. It's all we tend to see, but we have to re-focus on the fruit that God is producing through (or in spite of) the conflict. When Paul encountered some skirmishes in the church at Philippi, he helped them resolve conflict by focusing their minds and hearts on the bigger picture. In Philippians 1, he spoke of their participation in the gospel (v. 7); in chapter 2, he called them to a Christ-centered unity, appealing to them on the basis of the encouragement, consoling love, Spirit-filled resources, and deep compassion they had received from Christ (vv. 2–3); in chapter 3, they were challenged to emulate the godly character of mentors and shepherds (vv. 16–17); and in chapter 4, some leaders were admonished to resolve their differences because they had labored with Paul "side by side ... in the gospel" (v. 3). In a word, Paul helped the church get some altitude on their differences. This is great leadership!

Good leaders know that interpersonal conflicts quickly distract us from larger ministry goals. And where distractions exist, especially the emotionally-charged kind, it is difficult to keep our eyes on what God is doing to advance His kingdom. People need to be recalibrated. Without a vision of the grandeur of gospel ministry, disagreements become larger than life despite their petty origin. In a conflict, it's always wise to help others see where our differences fit in relationship to greater spiritual priorities. Moreover, Paul encouraged the leaders in Philippi to think in broader ministry terms so as to minimize the discouragement that inevitably follows conflict. Paul broadened the perspective of two women in the church who were in a serious dispute—serious enough to make it into his letter to that church. He told Euodia and Syntyche "to agree in the Lord." Then he added, "Yes, I ask you also, true companion, help these women, who have labored side by side with me in the gospel together with Clement and the rest of my fellow workers, whose names are in the book of life" (Phil 4:2–3). Interpersonal battles often result in sin, and sin generates fear. We can lose heart over the sins of others, fearing permanent damage to Christian fellowship. We can become stubborn, fearing the loss of reputation or control over an area of ministry. We often fear the loss of our credibility when a conflict brings out our worst. In those discouraging moments, it's a wonderful grace when someone reminds you of God's greater and broader work being done through your faithful partnership.

ENCOURAGE EVERYONE IN THE CONFLICT TO PARTICIPATE IN THE SOLUTION

A fifth principle to apply is this: everyone involved in the conflict should be engaged in problem solving. It's easy to find things to complain about. Leadership teams are often populated with very adept whiners—people who always seem to find the sour ball in a candy shop. They can point out problems in the church, but they offer no solutions. Everything seems bleak to them, and like hillside snipers who shoot and retreat, they sound off about everything that's "destroying the ministry" and yet offer no solutions. They can turn leadership meetings into a real downer. For someone who can point out a problem or conflict, my first question often is, *"So what do you think we ought to do? How can we go forward?"* It is crucial that those who lodge complaints actively engage in finding a solution. Otherwise, they will only be more critical when the solution falls short of their expectations, and they'll never learn to take responsibility for the outcome. In effect, they won't make good leaders.

When leading others through a conflict, I strongly urge everyone involved to fully engage in the process. This accomplishes three vital goals. First, it causes self-examination on the part of all involved. Conflicts are notorious arenas for accusation and blame-shifting. But tension in a conflict puts pressure on our own character so that what's inside of us gets exposed. Honest self-examination is crucial at such times. In order to avoid being exposed in a weakness, many leaders become silent participants. They attend meetings and gather all the data, but fear of being wrong keeps them from contributing anything of substance to the process. This is not an acceptable approach to problem solving. Only when we are willing to examine ourselves can we both glory in the Lord's faithfulness and grieve over our weaknesses.

Second, encouraging full participation allows all involved to maximize the use of their gifts. It is exciting to see the Holy Spirit use people uniquely to help resolve conflict. No one individual brings everything needed to solve problems. Some leaders—often the type-A personalities—will dominate tension-filled meetings, leaving the timid to wonder whether they can ever be used of the Lord at all! I prefer to engage everyone's personality and giftedness. Everyone is different and brings a level of spiritual maturity, gifting, and competence to resolving conflict. There are eight-cylinder leaders, twelve-cylinder leaders, and some who aren't firing on all the cylinders God has given them. When everyone submits to the Spirit of God, however, His wisdom begins to permeate the uniquely gifted people around the table. Stirring up the spiritual graces given to us by the Spirit brings great encouragement.

Third, I encourage all involved to take responsibility for the outcome and fallout. As leaders, we watch over souls. It is not helpful when we become frustrated in the struggle to resolve conflict, only to give up on the entire process. Worse, embattled sheep are sometimes given strong biblical correctives and left not knowing how to apply them practically. Resolving conflict is messy, and the temptation to be impatient and take shortcuts can be strong. But we must stay with the sheep throughout the process until our counsel is applied. This is how leaders take responsibility for the counsel they give, and it's how we model the very truth we are asking others to apply in a conflict. To admonish God's people without also bearing the weight of its impact on their lives turns shepherding into mere sheep herding. We must feed *and lead* our people. Walking with struggling sheep through their painful conflict as they apply our counsel is a safeguard against pride. Authority without responsibility is dangerous. Counsel becomes flippant and deep-seated issues of the heart are treated superficially.

Many leaders seem to glory in their ability to "reprove, rebuke and exhort" in sermons while letting others worry about the ongoing, close-range care of hurting sheep. But true shepherding takes into consideration how biblical principles are applied practically in people's lives. A faithful leader walks others through the impact of the truth on their particular problem, step by step. As a result, helping others resolve conflict goes beyond theory and platitudes. Biblical solutions are clearer and more thoughtful, principles are applied more faithfully, and anticipation of the "peace of Christ" ruling in our hearts is heightened. Moreover, going the distance in the peacemaking process forces us to evaluate the outcome biblically. What does God say about the fruit of restoration? Are we measuring ourselves against the biblical standard for living in harmony with one another? Have we truly resolved our conflict in a way that pleases Christ? Frequently answering these questions together compels us to unity and stimulates us to love one another more fervently.

CULTIVATE COMPASSION RATHER THAN CYNICISM

Another critical principle is to guard against cynicism. God calls us to be compassionate toward one another and patient when wronged (2 Tim 2:24). Leaders deal with a lot of heartache, often seeing people at their spiritual worst. And some under our care are actually stubborn mules in sheep's skin. It is tempting to become cynical about whether people can resolve their issues. When inundated with people problems, we can wrongly focus on the inconveniences, slights, misrepresentations, and unruly conduct of those we are trying to help. In our discouragement over having our efforts spurned once again, we are tempted to close our hearts to that person. We become compassionless toward them and cynical about their desire to change. Cynicism is unloving (1 Cor 13:7; 1 John 3:17)!

On the one hand, we must deal with the sins of others with a straightforward, tough love that speaks truth without flinching. On the other hand, our own personal struggles with besetting weaknesses should produce compassion for others. We understand the nature of spiritual battles. We grasp the sinner's profound, moment-by-moment need for sustaining grace. And we know that resolving conflict between offended parties is no walk in the park (Prov 18:19). God is patient with us, but He's also determined to root out our sinful tendencies. Some will soften under His chastening early on in the process. It's easy for us to have compassion on those more willing to change. But others will require God's "bit and bridle" to bring them under control (Ps 32:9). Still others may need to be taken by the Lord into a spiritual "desert" in order to bring them low and nurture a greater appetite for Him. Whatever means the Lord uses to refine His struggling saints, we must identify with their plight and express compassion in the crisis!

MAINTAIN OPEN ACCESS
TO THE LEADERSHIP

Don't hide from your congregation! The apostles referred to shepherds as those who were always in the midst of their sheep. Peter said, "Shepherd the flock of God *that is among you*" (1 Pet 5:2). Similarly, Paul says in 1 Thessalonians 2:7, "We were gentle *among you*." Be in their midst with open access. We may not be able to give details of all leadership meetings and decision-making processes, but integrity in the inside leads to transparency on the outside. Speak openly of the burden of leadership, yet follow it up with great encouragement about how the Lord is leading. Hide nothing that would promote Scripture, spiritually edify the people, and model how God's people deal with sin and conflict. And ask the congregation to regularly pray for both what they're able to know and what they cannot know. You can't tell the flock everything, for that would be to burden them with heavy specifics they weren't intended to carry. But when a leader's life and reasoning are open to anyone who is willing to learn and grow, sinful conflict has nowhere to go.

> *Lord, I pray for the ability to gain wisdom from Your Word for the shepherding of Your people, particularly in the midst of conflict. Help me learn from Your Word and from the mature counsel of those who have gone before us in ministry. May I carefully and patiently put into practice every wise principle from Your Word so that I too am edified through the process. Keep me humble, help me model deference, nurture within me the compassion of my Savior. Amen!*

11

WHEN LEADERS DEFECT

We went through a crisis in our church some years ago when a longtime staff member was exposed as having lived a shameless life of sin, stretching back for years. It was all exposed in one weekend. As I prepared Saturday night to announce the devastating news to our flock, I began to pray for Solomonic wisdom. The sermon I had prepared in the flow of our current study would have to be put on hold. I was facing a shepherding season I had not dealt with before, and the fallout of the crisis—given the years and level of betrayal—would surely be paralyzing to the ministry. I knew everyone would be shocked and deeply grieved, but some within our fellowship were about to relive the pain they felt over a decade earlier, before I came, when the senior pastor defaulted morally. There was no seminary class on how to deal with defection at this level. I had no script to follow. How was I going to navigate the fallout and help our people avoid slipping into despair and divisiveness? How would our ministry keep from shattering, and dishonoring the Lord? This particular Sunday morning would be like no other.

My children and their spouses asked to sit with me in the service. I wondered what message that would send to the church, being a bit unusual. Their love and support was comforting, but I was concerned that the church body might jump to conclusions, imagining a crisis in *my* life and ministry before they knew

157

anything. That morning's welcome and introduction to the service had to be worded very carefully. We couldn't simply carry on through the first thirty minutes as though nothing was looming, yet we also are a worshiping community who gathers to set our minds on Christ. I asked one of our staff who was introducing the service to say very specific words: *"We're going to open the service a little differently this morning. We're going to sing a couple hymns and then our pastor is going to come shepherd us through a very serious leadership issue."* First, I wanted the sheep to know that I was their shepherd, and that I was ready to walk with them as we face what they were about to discover. The leadership crisis did not involve any character issues in my life. Yet I also wanted to initially prepare them for a "serious leadership issue" that had come to light. Using that specific language let them know that we would have to seek the Lord together.

Leadership defection, whether moral or doctrinal, drives the church to the Scriptures. Such times force us to examine our attitudes, our character, and our tendency to become complacent in our walk with the Lord (1 Cor 4:3–5; Gal 6:4–5). While we pray for unity, harmony, and leadership integrity in our ministry, we also know that "the testing of [our] faith produces endurance" (Jas 1:3, NASB). As God protects the purity and unity of His people by exposing those who would destroy it, we are called to walk humbly before Him. Defection sobers a congregation. It causes the faithful to take their spiritual temperature and "see if there be any grievous way" in them (Ps 139:24). Churches do not often survive the destruction of leadership defection. It takes many months to work carefully through the issues, and usually several years before the ministry can gather for worship without painful reminders. Spiritual endurance is needed at these times, and God is generous with the wisdom essential to survival in the wake of a leadership crisis.

HOW TO ENDURE A LEADERSHIP DEFECTION

Not everyone in ministry will suffer the tragedy of a defecting or suddenly disqualified leader, but it does happen. Satan is always seeking to devour God's people (1 Pet 5:8)—to devour their effectiveness and destroy their faith—and if he can strike the shepherds of the church, he can scatter the sheep for many years after. In the wake of leadership defection, congregations become particularly vulnerable to certain temptations not experienced before. Emotional trauma distracts us from the Scriptures and we begin yearning for relief rather than fixing our eyes on the perfecter of our faith (Heb 12:2). We need robust biblical principles set as pillars in a crisis so that our response to a leadership defection is rightly sobered, humble, and Christ-exalting. On that Sunday morning, I taught four principles which must undergird our response and guard our hearts and minds. I then warned our congregation of five temptations that would rush upon them like a tidal wave in the months and perhaps years ahead.

THE CHURCH BELONGS TO THE LORD JESUS CHRIST

As soon as I discovered my associate's secret life of shame, I called a longtime mentor for wisdom and encouragement. I'll never forget his first words: *"This is a great thing!"* The comment caught me off guard. I asked, "Well, in what sense at all could this be a great thing?" He replied, "Up to this point, God has protected your people from greater evils while this man was in your midst. And now that he's been exposed there will be greater sobriety and spiritual fortitude in your people—greater usefulness for the gospel." It was timely counsel from a very seasoned soldier who had faced a number of similar situations.

This is *the* essential first principle. The Lord Jesus said, "I will build my church, and the gates of hell shall not prevail against it" (Matt 16:18). He is building His church. Whatever we face in the life of our church—whatever sinister inroads the enemy is able to gain—the ministry of the local church is not *our* ministry. Despite all her spots and wrinkles, the church belongs to the supreme Lord of the church, Jesus Christ. Our people need immediate recalibration in a crisis. This was not a time to become self-pitying and despondent as though sin *in* the camp means that God *has abandoned* the camp. Gross sin at the leadership level tempts remaining leaders to circle the wagons, take control, and react emotionally. It causes congregations to close ranks and cease ministering to others for fear of being hurt. We behave as though shocked that there could ever be "tares among the wheat" (Matt 13:25, NASB). But "the Lord knows those who are his" (2 Tim 2:19). He saved us "that he might present the church to himself in splendor, without spot or wrinkle or any such thing, that she might be holy and without blemish" (Eph 5:27). We are not yet what our Savior desires, but He is completing the work He began (Phil 1:6), and He will present us to Himself in the splendor of His power to conform us to His image.

GOD IS HOLY AND HE DESIRES A PURE CHURCH

Second, God is holy and He desires a pure church. In a crisis, the church is compelled to seek the Lord and tremble at His Word (Isa 66:2). God requires truth in the inner man (Ps 51:6). We believe the Scripture when it says, "Be sure your sin will find you out" (Num 32:23). Defectors always make "shipwreck of their faith" (1 Tim 1:19). God is holy and desires that His church be conformed to His holiness (1 Pet 1:15). An unholy leader of God's people is an assault on our spiritual sensibilities. Selfish defectors—savage wolves who shred the sheep—should not be given even a moment's welcome. And yet evangelicalism has seemed unwilling to deal definitively with unholy leaders and defectors. If they're popular, we excuse them. If they've made public apologies, we demand no ongoing, well-known fruit of repentance. If they're self-willed we re-label them "type-A personalities." And despite the arrogance of some younger leaders, we warn them while laying hands on them anyway. Defection among leaders— moral and doctrinal—will continue to be the trend if we do not recalibrate our ministries with the truth that God wants a pure church and will not cease to bring judgment to the house of God until she is spotless (1 Pet 4:17).

GOD'S WORD ALONE SANCTIFIES

Third, the church must remember that it is God's Word alone that sanctifies. Whether we are at peace or in turmoil, God's people should fly to the Scriptures. Jesus pinpointed the ground and power of His sanctifying work when He prayed that His Father would "sanctify them in the truth; your word is truth" (John 17:17). In a crisis, we run to God's Word alone. The spiritual defection of a leader signals a departure from the truth in that person's life. God's people cannot remain faithful and discerning if their reaction to a crisis is to neglect the very source of truth— the departure from which as what led to the crisis in the first place. Yet, in seasons of trial we often begin to protect ourselves; we fail to ask God for wisdom (Jas 1:5; 4:2); and we wrangle about issues with mere opinions. Since it is the power of the Holy Spirit through His Word alone that renews our minds and helps us discern truth from error (Heb 4:12; 5:14), we must reject speculations and human solutions. The preaching of God's Word is central in our corporate worship, so that even a crisis at the leadership level should not be allowed to distract us from the transforming power of truth. When we are spiritually starving from heartache, what we need most is food for our souls!

GUARDING THE CHURCH DEMANDS
THAT WE GUARD OUR HEARTS

Finally, in the midst of a crisis we must watch over our hearts and "take every thought captive to obey Christ" (2 Cor 10:5).

Fertile ground for sin comes from spiritual neglect or hypocrisy. When counseling his sons, Solomon went straight to the core issue: "Keep your heart with all vigilance, for from it flow the springs of life" (Prov 4:23). The inner life needs constant care to bring our thoughts, motives, affections, will, and emotions under the perfect instruction of Christ. We want our corporate body life to be in the place of God's maximum blessing, so we must as individuals strive for it. A tiny bit of yeast affects the entire lump of dough (1 Cor 5:6; Gal 5:9). Moral and doctrinal defection rarely occurs quickly, nor does it usually permeate the entire congregation all at once. It is much more subtle, hard to identify at first, and frequently traceable to a particular leader whose life slowly unraveled into spiritual neglect and hypocrisy. Wherever we establish spiritual vaccinations in our own hearts, we will strengthen the corporate body's overall immune system against ultimate defection.

ALERT TO THE FALLOUT OF LEADERSHIP DEFECTION

When a leader fails or a church splits, the sheep inevitably face unique and powerful temptations likely not experienced before. We must prepare our people before these strong enticements come upon them. When I stood before our congregation to lead them through this very painful defection of one of our own, I warned them of five temptations that would surely rise up within them. These would be formidable and not to be treated lightly.

SINFUL ANGER AND VENGEANCE

First, in the midst of a leadership crisis the people will be tempted to become angry and vengeful. Mentally and emotionally trauma-tized people—even the most godly—are prone to let their sense of betrayal rule them. Fear of being further duped and betrayed by those you trusted begins to consume your thought life. The temptation to retaliate is very intense! Scripture is about as blunt on this forbidden response as it can be. Romans 12:19 says, "Beloved, never avenge yourselves, but leave it to the wrath of God, for it is written, 'Vengeance is mine, I will repay, says the Lord.'" When is it right to return evil for evil? Never! Why? It is God who will repay. "Vengeance is mine, I will repay, says the Lord." Betrayal seems to be the one area where believers assume God will allow exceptions to this command.

Our culture glorifies vengeance. It has become a virtue, and anything less than sticking it to others who have done you wrong is a sign of weakness. True Christianity is countercultural. We are called to "overcome evil with good" (Rom 12:21). Having reached out to others only to be mistreated and spurned, we should reach out in love yet again, risking the same mistreatment (Luke 6:29). Here is precisely where we often stumble. To forgive is to be most like our Savior. To reach out knowing that we may get rejected repeatedly is what it means to "leave it to the wrath of God." God knows every detail. He is intimately acquainted with the motives of every heart. And when every soul stands before God, all betrayals, slanders, injustices, and mistreatments will be brought to light and judged against the standard of God's holy perfections (Prov 16:2; Luke 8:17; 1 Cor 4:5; Heb 4:13). He knows every motive, and His wrath is perfectly just. The church must flee the temptation to retaliate against failed leaders. No human court is able to render an unbiased verdict. Moreover, if a defector remains unrepentant, his trouble with his Maker will have only just begun.

UNCHECKED SUSPICION

The second temptation is unchecked suspicion. As has often been declared by a seasoned pastor to pastors, "Time and truth go hand in hand." Not only does betrayal open up vulnerability to vengeance, it also paves the way for a culture of suspicion. Again, in order to protect ourselves from further pain and loss, we instantly become investigators, prosecuting everyone else's motives which we assume are sinister. One man said to me, "How can we trust you as elders when this guy went undetected for so long?" I simply replied, "We have to trust the Lord. There was no sign of it. If there had been a sign of it we would have dealt with it. When we saw the first sign of it, he was gone." We ought to ask instead, *"Where's my heart? What's the Lord doing in this?"* You will not be able to go before the Lord and say, *"Well, I was suspicious and turned myself away from ministry, Lord, but I had just cause—a person I trusted failed me."* We must remember that God is sovereign, even over evil that comes against us.

Being victimized by others does not truly make us a victim. The Lord never fails His people. He ordains all things for our spiritual best, and works to carry out every detail of His flawless plan to conform us to the image of His Son (Rom 8:28–29). It may take some time for an offended brother or sister to be at ease with trusting someone who has betrayed them or defected. Trusting their yet-proven repentance and character is one thing. Overcoming their betrayal with the kindness of spiritual blessings instead is the power of the gospel (1 Pet 3:9).

USING ANOTHER'S SIN AS LICENSE

A third temptation is to use another's sin as license for your own: *"Well, if men I respect are not able to remain faithful, then there cannot be any hope of my faithfulness, so why continue to battle?"* In the wake of leadership defection, we are tempted to become discouraged, giving in to temptations we have been resisting for some time. Our most honored leaders are supposed to be above reproach. When a great mentor defects, our flesh rages with a thousand excuses and cries of injustice. We can even become initially self-righteous as another way of protecting ourselves from vulnerability. We stand with fierce indignation over a fallen leader, but given enough time our "righteous indignation" gets exposed as deep-seated resentment for having curbed the flesh while our teachers made no such sacrifice. Like Asaph, we become envious of the apparent "freedom" others have to get away with sinning (Ps 73:1–14).

Almost without warning, our hearts descend into petty resentment. At that point, we are in grave danger of opening our hearts to the enemy and using the sin of others to justify giving in ourselves. But we are reminded in 2 Corinthians 5:10 that "we must all appear before the judgment seat of Christ, so that each one may receive what is due for what he has done in the body, whether good or evil." We will stand alone before the Lord of glory and give an account for everything we have thought, said, or done. That will not be a time for excusing sin because we were angry at the poor example of others. We cannot say, *"Lord, I trusted a leader and he defected and left me confused and despondent."* We may indeed have been severely provoked, leading to strong temptation. But our choice to yield to the enticement was caused by our love for satisfying our lusts (Jas 1:13–14).

SELF-PITY AND DISILLUSIONMENT

Another temptation that will come is that of becoming disillusioned and plunging into self-pity. The defection of a leader can bring a ministry to its knees. Otherwise peace-filled churches are suddenly thrown into a season of backbiting, unresolved bitterness, public rancor, private slander, and every kind of evil. Timid sheep can't handle the tension, and so they begin demanding reconciliation without wanting to work through a process involving further conflict. When issues take a long time to be resolved, people become weary and want to give up (Gal 6:9; 2 Thess 3:13; Heb 12:3). Self-pity is common in the fallout of a leadership crisis, and if unchecked, can lead a ministry into the deep valley of disillusionment.

When a church body becomes collectively despondent, the power of the gospel is muted. Preaching—even really good exposition—begins to sound harsh and academic. Once vibrant praise and adoration in song becomes mere ventriloquism, moving our mouths to words which are not from genuine hearts before God. We repeat questions such as, *"How can this be? How could this have happened?"* but we stop turning to God for the answers. It is essential during the healing process that we "seek first the kingdom of God" (Matt 6:33) and "set [our] minds on things that are above, not on things that are on earth" (Col 3:2). We may not know what to pray for as we ought, but "the Spirit helps us in our weakness" and "intercedes for us with groanings too deep for words" (Rom 8:26). We might come to the place where we despair "of life itself" as Paul did (2 Cor 1:8). But we must remember to lay our fears and burdens at the Lord's gentle and compassionate feet (1 Pet 5:7).

FEAR OF REPROACH FROM OUTSIDE THE CHURCH

Finally, I warned our church of the temptation to fear the reproach of those from other ministries or from the community. Unfortunately, some churches seem to glory in another ministry's scandal. Perhaps they want to capitalize on the bleeding and gather up the stray sheep to increase their numbers. Sometimes the bad news about your church gives other ministries a sense of satisfaction rooted in a resentment toward your doctrine or practice. And that's just the "friendly fire," so to speak. Many in the community will use your crisis as evidence that your church is disingenuous and a pariah in the community. The temptation is to fear such reproaches. But we must return to the principles of faithful ministry which have long since strengthened the church and blessed the lives of sinners saved by grace.

EPILOGUE: ENCOURAGEMENTS ALONG THE WAY

In the midst of discouraging times, the Lord graciously brings encouragement. During the most difficult months, in God's kind providence we received several notes from people who took the above principles and warnings seriously. The Lord used them to bring encouragement our way in some of our most heartache-filled hours. One saint wrote, "Even in the greatest sorrow and tragedy the hand of God truly is so very beautiful. Know that we stand firm in the joy of knowing Him. Loving this church family and standing close to our Lord in prayer alongside you leaders." They were teaching me!

Another one wrote, "This situation serves as a reminder to us of how Christ is the Head of His church, the true Shepherd of His sheep and the One in control. The under-shepherds must keep in mind that the Great Shepherd is actively at work in His flock, accomplishing His good purposes."

"God is good all the time," another one said. "His truth does keep us free from sin, so thank you for being faithful in teaching us His Word."

And another: "Pastor, God's Word convicted me of my own hypocrisy and need for constant genuine repentance and sanctification." My vitality was returning.

One wrote, "When we take our eyes off the face of God and stop seeking His will for our lives in the illumination of His Word, there really are no boundaries on what we might tolerate, rationalize, and accept as truth." What a great statement from someone in the church!

Humbled and pliable, one person wrote, "Thank you for shining the truth of God's Word into our hearts. Praying that God will give me the grace to rightfully repent of sinful areas with a true, godly sorrow."

These encouragements did not come immediately, nor all at once. But each expression of grace was perfectly timed and tailor-made by God to uplift and edify our elders.

> *Lord, thank You for the way You minister to us through Your church in time past, and through Your Word, and by Your Spirit. These are gifts to us because otherwise we're just fearful, timid strugglers. We get*

into these situations and sometimes doubt, "Is it all me? Do I just need to get out of ministry?" Lord, may we never answer our own questions with our own answers. May we go to Your Word and ask the questions You ask and answer those questions with what You say. May Christ, the Head of His church, be the shining light in all our ministries. Lord, be the One we turn to, for You alone have words of eternal life. Drive these truths deep into our hearts, and encourage us by Your Spirit. We pray in Your name. Amen.

12

THE LEADER AS
WATCHMAN

When I accepted the call to be the pastor of my own flock, I had no idea what to expect. During seminary, students would try to imagine the first couple of years in a new church, and we speculated on the length of the oft-mentioned "honeymoon period." I had an advantage over most students in that I gained some years of experience as an associate pastor in a very large, multi-staffed church while in school. Still, without actually bearing the full weight and burden of a senior pastor it was difficult knowing how to prepare. Just before leaving Grace Community Church, Sun Valley, California to assume the senior pastorate where I serve now, I asked John MacArthur to give me a couple of final tips before I left. Without hesitating he said, "You're going to find that your ministry as an associate pastor at Grace Community has been quite private and protected. But when you take the role as senior shepherd, your ministry will suddenly become very public. So be on your guard!" I've been reminded of that advice repeatedly throughout the challenges of ministry. After seventeen years "in the saddle," as they say, I'm beginning to understand what a "public" ministry is like. It is loaded with hazards, pitfalls, challenges, and difficulties that no one would choose to face were it not a divine calling.

The leadership team of godly men around me is a grace-gift from the Lord. They encourage me, pray for me, labor to exhaustion alongside me, and I couldn't accomplish the work without their gifted and faithful service. There are, however, a unique set of burdens carried by the one on whom the other leaders and congregation depend for their feeding and care. If I lack spiritual courage, the others can more easily falter. Were I to fail morally, the devastation would outlast that of anyone else in the leadership. If my family relationships were imploding because of gross spiritual neglect or hypocrisy on my part, the effects on the flock are more deeply felt. Knowing the seriousness of my leadership responsibility has served to make me alert and sober-minded about this awesome privilege. Without a constant sense of urgency and sobriety, leaders become vulnerable to various pitfalls common to those in positions of spiritual responsibility.

The task of the modern-day, literal shepherd in the Middle East, tending his flock, is an extremely burdensome work. He is most often pictured calmly walking beside his flock through a valley or along some peaceful hillside. But a shepherd who understands the gravity of the job is anything but calm! His eyes constantly search the horizon for approaching dangers. His sheep are vulnerable to inclement weather with sudden flash floods that sweep through the valley. The constant threat of predators—lions, bears, wolves—that can swiftly and easily shred the sheep are an ever-constant danger around every ridge. Along with such things comes the challenge of the nature of sheep. They are the most difficult animal to provide for and protect. They are easily sent into a panic, they are restless around each other, they have little sense, and one will blindly follow the other into the path of death. Richard Mayhue calls the shepherd a "Spiritual Sentinel."[1] These

---

1   Richard L. Mayhue, "Watching and Warning," Chapter 20, John MacArthur and The Master's Seminary Faculty, *Pastoral Ministry: How to Shepherd Biblically* (Nashville, TN: Thomas Nelson, 2005), 279.

sentinels are "not only approved workmen (2 Tim 2:15), but also *unashamed watchmen*."[2] The shepherd is called a watchman for good reason! He can never neglect the safety of his flock, nor be indifferent or reckless concerning their constant need for food and shelter. If he becomes timid and self-preserving, he will run at the first sign of trouble, and the sheep are doomed. If he miscalculates the seriousness of his duties and becomes careless or casual, the flock will not be spared. Mayhue sets the tone by saying, "In a life-and-death situation, he must alertly tend the flock like a vigilant watchman protects his city."[3]

Besides the character and motivation problems discussed in Chapter 6, shepherds must be careful not to fall into other sinful leadership patterns—sins of neglect, indifference, and recklessness. Such things devastate our effectiveness, create distrust and suspicion, and leave the people without the tools for discerning good from evil. The ministry is not a place for the timid, the flippant, or the naïve. Every shepherd who understands what's at stake stays far away from anything that might dull his spiritual senses.

SELF-PRESERVATION

When Paul was instructing Timothy on the urgency of pastoral courage, he warned him of three particular dangers: (1) forgetting our spiritual heritage and calling; (2) fearing man rather than God; (3) failing to uphold the truth above our own interests. Ephesus was a great church to be serving in, but there were some obvious challenges that put Timothy on edge. First, he was a young pastor charged with feeding and leading a flock where some of the members were quite a bit older than he and didn't respond to his leadership very warmly (1 Tim 4:12). Second, some men had come into the church eloquently speaking "strange doctrines" (1 Tim

---

2   Ibid.

3   Ibid., 280.

1:3) and having a detrimental influence on the purity and unity of the fellowship (1 Tim 1:20; 6:20–21). By the time Paul wrote the second epistle to his young disciple, Timothy needed encouragement to remain strong and faithful in the battle.

REMEMBER YOUR SPIRITUAL HERITAGE

First, Paul reminds this young pastor of his spiritual heritage and the divine calling on his life: "I am reminded of your sincere faith, a faith that dwelt first in your grandmother Lois and your mother Eunice and now, I am sure, dwells in you as well. For this reason I remind you to fan into a flame the gift of God which is in you through the laying on of my hands" (2 Tim 1:5–6). This principle is so important when spiritual courage is needed. Spiritual leaders must remember that they serve in a long line of soldiers who have weathered the storms of ministry. Timothy had been blessed to have a mother and grandmother who loved Christ and taught him to fear God. He was saved in God's mercy and then called into the gospel ministry. This was no time to lose resolve, to stop battling for the souls of men and women. On the contrary, there was no more urgent time and place than when and where Timothy was serving. Losing his nerve in the midst of criticism and persecution was not the character of a true watchman. Timothy needed a reminder that he came from privileged stock, and was called and chosen by God for ministry impact. All spiritual leaders need the constant encouragement of ministry camaraderie. Peter reminded the heavily persecuted elders scattered throughout the Asian provinces that he was a "fellow elder," and that he goes before them as a "witness of the sufferings of Christ" and "a partaker in the glory that is going to be revealed" (1 Pet 5:1). The writer of Hebrews strengthened the resolve of God's people with a kind of "Hall of Faith" (Heb 11:4–40), calling it a great "cloud of witnesses" (Heb 12:1). We can't simply walk away from our duties as watchmen. Many such guardians and shepherds have gone before us, giving us a pattern to follow.

FEAR GOD, NOT MEN

Second, another important encouragement from Paul was for Timothy to fear God and trust in His power:

> For God gave us a spirit not of fear but of power and love and self-control. Therefore, do not be ashamed of the testimony about our Lord, nor of me his prisoner, but share in suffering for the gospel by the power of God … which is why I suffer as I do. But I am not ashamed, for I know whom I have believed, and I am convinced that he is able to guard until that Day what has been entrusted to me. (2 Tim 1:7–8, 12)

Notice that it is the power of God and deep conviction that kept Paul from self-preservation. As I stated in Chapter 4, hirelings abandon their post at the first sign of trouble, a fault worthy of severe rebuke by our Lord (John 10:11–15). Self-preservation at all costs is a weakness, not a virtue. When we're godly we have nothing to fear; when integrity rules our hearts we become as courageous as lions (Prov 28:1). If we're going to be faithful watchmen, we must realize that our responsibility is more than mere titles. We're called to do more than just feed the sheep and hear them say, "Great sermon!" It is our charge also to lead and protect our people by being more concerned about where *God* is taking them than any human agenda. Fearing God means that we are willing to suffer (2 Tim 1:8; 2:3); it means that our hearts are immovably grounded in the power of God to save us and make us instruments for the gospel (2 Tim 1:9–11); we become unashamed servants of the living God in whom we have confidence to guard the fruit of our labors until He returns for His people in glory (2 Tim 1:12). "The fear of the Lord must teach a young man wisdom, or he is barred from the pastorate; the grace of God must mature his spirit, or he had better tarry till power be given him from on high."[4]

I know the internal turmoil that results whenever ministry issues demand that I stand alone on the minority side of some conflict. The temptation is to conciliate out of fear and feelings of isolation. We never make good decisions when the fear of man is ruling our hearts. Timothy was getting it from all sides, and his pastoral courage was weakening. The constant threat of Roman persecution escalating under Nero, hostility from some who resented Timothy's leadership, and the sophisticated, high-powered doctrinal assaults from false teachers were taking their toll.[5] Fear of man can rush in suddenly under such pressure, but we must not succumb to the snare. Satan stirs up our circumstances with compounding trouble because he knows that our minds will often dwell there in worry, fretting over every detail so that we become distracted and confused. (We're warned about this tendency in Matthew 6:25–34.) We should take our cues from the apostle Paul, who said that his greatest fear was not persecution, but that the sheep would be "led astray from the simplicity and purity of devotion to Christ" (2 Cor 11:3, NASB). Leaving our people vulnerable to Satan's devices has to become our greatest concern as vigilant watchmen. "To do less would result in hollow ministry, invite Christ's displeasure ... and endanger the spiritual health of the flock. Their blood would be on our hands."[6]

UPHOLD THE TRUTH

Finally, Timothy is encouraged to uphold the truth above his own interests. Proclaiming the truth boldly will get spiritual leaders in

---

4   C. H. Spurgeon, *Lectures to My Students* (Grand Rapids, MI: Zondervan Publishing House, 1954), 13.

5   John MacArthur, *The MacArthur Study Bible* (Nashville, TN: Word Publishing, 1997), 1875.

6   Richard Mayhue, "Watching and Warning," 283.

a lot of trouble with those who resist it. After I had been preaching for two years at our church, I noticed a drastic increase in counseling and a general agitation on the part of some who had been in the church for several years. One couple took me to lunch and told me that "the church just didn't 'feel' the way it used to." When I asked them whether they had doctrinal or philosophy of ministry concerns, they denied any but couldn't really put their finger on what the problem was. I knew the issue right away. When the Word of God is clearly and boldly proclaimed, the Holy Spirit goes to work on the hearts of His people (Heb 4:12).

Many leaders and shepherds, when facing the normal restlessness of the sheep under conviction, begin to avoid certain doctrines and pointed texts that may incite more discomfort and more anonymous notes from the congregation. Paul reminded Timothy that we mustn't put a dimmer-switch on Scripture. His admonishments are frequent and inspiring: "Follow the pattern of the sound words" (2 Tim 1:13); "Guard the good deposit entrusted to you" (2 Tim 1:14); "Present yourself to God as one approved … who has no need to be ashamed, rightly handling the word of truth" (2 Tim 2:15); "Continue in what you have learned and have firmly believed, knowing from whom you learned it" (2 Tim 3:14); "I charge you in the presence of God and of Christ Jesus … Preach the word; be ready in season and out of season; reprove, rebuke, and exhort, with complete patience and teaching" (2 Tim 4:1–2). God's watchmen work hard to set personal interests aside so that the central issue in the life of the church is always the truth! Anything less is "biblically unthinkable and spiritually unconscionable."[7]

SERIOUS MISCALCULATIONS

It's tragic when young men, training for the ministry, get their notions about church leadership from today's evangelical

---

7 Ibid.

landscape. The megachurch leaders of today are like executives, CEOs who happen to know a great deal about marketing and public relations and not very much about biblical ministry. They treat shepherding problems like middle-management issues to be dealt with by hiring and firing, reorganization, and popularity contests. Other churches, especially those with a post-evangelical bent, look at ministry as a haven for disenfranchised, disheartened rebels who simply need a "community" where they feel loved. Doctrinal confusion, moral weakness, and raw emotionalism is not only expected by the leadership in these environments, it is strongly encouraged as what is supposedly the more honest, humble, and virtuous path.

Taking our leadership cues from seeker-driven or emerging churches is a devastating miscalculation of the ministry. Without the powerful proclamation of transcendent truth no one can ever be sanctified (John 17:17). Without godly shepherds who equip the saints to grow in Christ and labor for Him, there is only moral debility and spiritual defenselessness against error (Eph 4:12–16). Young men will often use their first pastorate as a testing ground for any methodology that promises them "success"—the kind they have mistakenly coveted during their years of training. Instead, we must anchor our ministry ideals to the truth! When Paul was nearing the end of his third missionary journey and hurrying to get to Jerusalem, he stopped over in Miletus (Acts 20:15–17), meeting with the elders from the church in Ephesus where he had once spent three years planting and growing the ministry. It was a desperate time for the churches, a time fraught with severe and frequent hazards. The truth was making a dent in the kingdom of darkness, but truth-haters were infiltrating the churches and seeking to devour the sheep. Paul wanted to exhort the Ephesian elders to stay alert and be watchful. He gave them an unforgettable view of the ministry that would keep them from becoming reckless, casual, or naïve.

LIVE FOR ETERNAL PRIORITIES

Paul's amazing habit of looking at his leadership from an eternal perspective is what made his life and preaching so compelling to other leaders and their churches. He unflinchingly told the elders of Ephesus that though the Spirit was strongly indicating his imprisonment and torture in Jerusalem (Acts 20:22–23), he did not count his life as "of any value nor as precious" to himself (Acts 20:24). He had a course to "finish," a ministry "received from the Lord Jesus, to testify solemnly of the gospel of the grace of God" (Acts 20:24). Paul was always setting his heart and mind on "things that are above, not on things that are on the earth" (Col 3:2). As spiritual leaders, if we cling to the comforts of earth and view the ministry as a channel through which we will enjoy the "gusto" of this life, we cannot possibly discern the dangers. What will we do when the schemes of Satan are too subtle for a surface treatment? The shepherd who sits idle, thoroughly engrossed in his slice of earthly pie, does the sheep much harm. Paul wanted to be "innocent of the blood of all men" (Acts 20:26, NASB), which made him think about truth, souls, heaven, hell, sin, Satan's lies, and Christ's glory! If we count our lives as more dear than truth, we will foster the same in the sheep. People will become spiritually atrophied, their level of discernment reduced to surface platitudes, and their lives shattered by the clever deceptions of sin.

GUARD YOURSELF AND OTHERS

I receive letters and emails regularly, asking about certain books and teachers that have become popular among evangelicals. I'm amazed at the speed and flippancy with which error sweeps through churches today. It's as though people are desperately longing for something, anything, that will momentarily pull them up out of their spiritual doldrums. When William P. Young's book, *The Shack*, another "Christian fiction" (whatever that is), was released, it quickly rose to fever-pitch in churches all over the United States and Europe. It was rightly criticized by many as full of unbiblical notions about the Trinity, salvation, sanctification, etc., but these discerning reviewers met with widespread and fierce opposition by professing evangelicals. In spite of the book's dangerously errant theological assumptions, Christians everywhere have shockingly given it "two thumbs up." Once again, the latest "totally-changed-my-life" fad was served up to a voracious evangelicalism hardly stopping to take a breath.

Paul set his heart on knowing and living the truth (Ezra 7:10) so that his mind was sharp enough to recognize a wolf in sheep's clothing. Christians today seem perennially seduced by human opinions and experience offered as the answer to life's trials, even though we give weekly affirmations in corporate worship about the sufficiency of Scripture. How can one man's story of a fictional encounter with fictional deities provide more comfort than real revelation from the one true and living God? Do believers now prefer fiction to divine revelation? Sadly, they do. The reason is because it's easier (or so we think) to fashion thoughts about God around our experiences rather than to submit to the truth. We make God fit Himself through our grid, respond to our burdens in our timing, and allow us enough pride to save face in the event our weaknesses are exposed. Beware the novel that pretends fiction with a Trojan Horse of lies against the truth. Fiction can be fun, but eternity is no fiction!

"Be on guard for yourselves and for all the flock" (Acts 20:28, NASB). I chased the Greek verb for "be on guard" around the New Testament and found twenty-one uses: fourteen are warnings about dangerous error, four speak of calling someone to give a careful hearing, and three are a charge to heed Scripture. A similar Greek word is used in verse 31 and is translated "be alert." Some leaders don't see any dangers because their *own* spiritual vitality is in peril. They don't recognize weakening influences because they're not experiencing the Spirit's sanctifying influence on a daily basis; and many lead their own people right into dangerous error. In *Lectures to My Students*, Charles Spurgeon begins with the chapter, "The Minister's Self-Watch," which includes this assessment: "[The minister's] pulse of vital godliness must beat strongly and regularly; his eye of faith must be bright; his foot of resolution must be firm; his hand of activity must be quick; his whole inner man must be in the highest degree of sanity."[8]

A good leader keeps his life pure and clean so that his spiritual eyesight remains sharp and his wisdom is applied with insight and depth (1 Tim 1:5–7; 1 Thess 5:21–22; Heb 5:14). If I am not growing, I can't give real answers to those I lead. As only Spurgeon can say it,

> I can only weep and agonize for souls in my own renewed nature, therefore must I watchfully maintain the tenderness which was in Christ Jesus. It will be vain for me to stock my library, or organize societies, or project schemes, if I neglect the culture of myself; for books, and agencies, and systems, are only remotely the instruments of my holy calling; my own spirit, soul, and body, are my nearest machinery for sacred service; my spiritual faculties, and my inner life, are my battle axe and weapons of war.[9]

LEAD AS A GOOD STEWARD

It is a serious miscalculation to think that the people of God are ours to do with as we please. The sheep are the "church of God, which he obtained with his own blood" (Acts 20:28). The Spirit of God has made us "overseers" to care for God's people. A man who sees himself as a steward of ministry privileges doesn't live to please the people, or fill his bank account, or become a popular circuit speaker. He's concerned with pleasing the one "who enlisted him as a soldier" (2 Tim 2:4, NASB). Every time the Scriptures speak of the people being God's "possession," I begin to tremble.

---

8   Spurgeon, *Lectures to My Students*, 13.

9   Ibid., 7–8.

I know that my many frailties need much covering grace from the Lord for the ministry to go forward with any effectiveness. Wherever I try to put my signature on the work of ministry or lead so as to earn personal trophies, the care of God's people suffers and they become vulnerable. Spiritual leaders must always direct attention away from themselves in order to exalt Christ. Paul and his band of church planters wanted to be regarded "as servants of Christ and stewards of the mysteries of God" (1 Cor 4:1). This perspective removes all lesser concerns and trivial pursuits, and it elevates the need for faithfulness (1 Cor 4:2).

KNOW THE CERTAINTY OF TROUBLE

The elders of Ephesus were left with a sobering message from their mentor. In effect, he told them that savage wolves were waiting for his departure before they made their move against the church (Acts 20:29). These vulnerable leaders were never to doubt the certainty of coming trouble, but were to remain alert and follow the example of the seasoned soldiers who had taught them: "Therefore be alert, remembering that for three years I did not cease night or day to admonish everyone with tears" (Acts 20:31). Sober-minded leaders know that wherever truth is proclaimed, Satan will launch a counter-offensive. When a shepherd doesn't think the ministry is all that susceptible to error, that is when it is most vulnerable.

The Scriptures always portray false teachers as deceptive and cunning, "disguising themselves as apostles of Christ" (2 Cor 11:13). Jesus warned that they come to us "in sheep's clothing" (Matt 7:15) rather than being easy to spot. Their lies are "secretly" introduced (2 Pet 2:1) as teachings compatible with orthodoxy *with only the slightest of nuances*. When it came to the church at Ephesus, Paul didn't hesitate to label these false leaders "savage wolves" (Acts 20:29, NASB), pack hunters who stalk their prey by sending out a single wolf to increase the element of stealth and surprise. While unsuspecting sheep are drawn to the one, the entire pack lies in wait, ferociously[10] exploiting the opportunity to destroy a life and scatter the others. Iranaeus bluntly unmasked the trickery of error:

> Error, indeed, is never set forth in its naked deformity, lest, being thus exposed, it should at once be detected. But it is craftily decked out in an attractive dress, so as, by its outward form, to make it appear to the inexperienced ... more true than the truth itself.[11]

We are never to be lulled into the belief that subtle lies against the truth are not at work in our midst, countering the Word of God and seeking to gain a destructive advantage over the unsuspecting. I tell my congregation often that though our church has been blessed with long seasons where truth is flourishing, Satan will never stop until he has "not spar[ed] the flock" (Acts 20:29). He never rests in the preparation and sending of an army of liars for deceiving the church. Paul minced no words with the Ephesian elders: "And from among your own selves will arise men speaking twisted things, to draw away the disciples after them" (Acts 20:30). While Satan is introducing hypocrites into the congregation, he sows petty discord among believers to weaken their defenses and strip them of any resolve to fight. When spiritual determination is at its lowest, Satan tempts us with the notion that tolerance, for the sake of peace, is the highest of virtues.

Spurgeon once said, "Complicity with error will take from the best of men the power to enter any successful protest against

---

10   Paul's use of "savage" here is the word *barus*, meaning "fierce," "heavy," or "ferocious." Some translations actually render it "grievous." It fittingly carries the idea of the weighty, devastating ruin that comes to the people of God through false teachers.

11   *Iraneaus Against Heresies*, preface to bk. 1, in vol. 1 of *The Writings of Iranaeus*, in *Ante-Nicene Christian Library*, (Grand Rapids, MI: Eerdmans [n.d.]), 5:2.

it."[12] False teachers learn our lingo, they "look" and "act" like Christians, and when the moment is right they speak "twisted things" designed to "draw away the disciples after them" (Acts 20:30). Perhaps it's an almost imperceptible resistance to God's authority, or a consistent questioning of well-established doctrines. Sometimes it begins with casting doubt on the Bible's trustworthiness while introducing the writings of unorthodox teachers. Some men simply play fast and loose with the Scriptures, offering subjective interpretations that sound "logical" to the naïve. Given enough time, these subtleties become full-blown heresies that capture and devour the sheep, and if possible, even other leaders. We cannot afford to take a casual approach in dealing with error. Where truth is strongly taught, error has a difficult time taking root. Tozer said it this way: "Moral power has always accompanied definitive beliefs."[13] In Revelation 2:14–15 the Lord Himself indicted the church in Pergamum for tolerating the errors of idolatry and immorality. This is serious business! We must not miscalculate our sober responsibility as watchmen over the flock of God. Like Paul, we must commend our people "to God and to the word of his grace" which is our only power against unholy and destructive errors (Acts 20:32). The work is one of sacrifice and strenuous labor (vv. 33–35), but we must keep in mind that to pour ourselves out for others is to follow Christ, who said, "It is more blessed to give than to receive" (v. 35).

My God and Father, the task of a watchman is more formidable than I'm capable of handling. Striving for holiness in my own life is battle enough, but to

12   Charles Spurgeon, "Notes," *The Sword and the Trowel* (October 1888), as quoted in John MacArthur, *Ashamed of the Gospel: When the Church Becomes Like the World* (Wheaton, IL: Crossway Books, 1993), 224.

13   "The Importance of Sound Doctrine," in *Man—The Dwelling Place of God*, (n.d.), www.worldinvisible.com/library/tozer/5j00.0010/5j00.0010.37.htm (accessed January, 2005).

take responsibility for Your people is too much for any man to bear. I am in desperate need of discernment, keen spiritual eyesight, courage no matter the cost, and supernatural strength to hold fast the word of life. Grant me understanding as I study and teach Your truth. Ground my convictions so that I fear You rather than men. Amen.

PART

3

THE DEVELOPMENT
OF LEADERSHIP

13

IDENTIFYING THE RAW MATERIALS

While participating in a defensive military exercise some years ago, my job was to provide radar air-traffic support to combat pilots as they engaged "bogeys." Basically, I guided them toward enemy aircraft during a modern-day dogfight. During this particular exercise, the scenario called for the simulation of a badly damaged fighter, low on fuel and carrying one remaining weapon, to radio my post looking for instructions back to base. I began to give him coordinates to get him home, but was interrupted by the battle commander on my frequency telling the pilot to turn around and drop his remaining weapon on enemy targets. "Excuse me, say again sir," the pilot replied with confusion. The commander radioed back with the same order—emphatically, I might add. Needless to say, because of the pilot's low fuel he couldn't get home. He obeyed the order, simulating an ejection somewhere very close to enemy territory. At the debriefing, I'll never forget the colonel's answer when I asked why we would risk a pilot just to deliver one more weapon. "Pilots are expendable!" He said it so abruptly and without hesitation. The point was very clear: the good of the whole always trumps individual interests. Applied to the spiritual realm, good leaders realize that their usefulness is in the hands of God, and they never see themselves as indispensable to the work. This is the beginning of the raw materials necessary for developing good leadership skills.

ARE WE IRREPLACEABLE?

No one is so vital that he can't be replaced! If the Lord "is able from … stones to raise up children" for Himself (Matt 3:9), He can surely develop spiritual leaders for His people. One of the raw materials needed in a good leader/shepherd is a right view of himself. Many elder boards and leadership teams are dysfunctional because of men who have taken themselves too seriously, believing that the ministry would absolutely crumble without them. They are highly offended when their ideas aren't lavishly supported, they promote their own pet ministries at every opportunity, and they talk often about their impact on people's lives. Secretly, these "irreplaceable" leaders think highly of their gifts in comparison to those around them. When our elders see the early signs of this kind of bravado in a young man, we refrain from giving them spiritual responsibility. We want to work with those who know that every day of spiritual leadership is another day in the shining sun of God's gracious love (1 Cor 4:7).

There are a few other basic premises that help us in the leadership development process. Some men in the church have never seriously considered serving in a leadership role because they don't see their own potential. For a variety of understandable reasons (lowly view of abilities, subdued personality, willingness to follow, etc.), there are those who have never envisioned themselves taking on spiritual responsibility. Wise leaders can see latent giftedness and leadership strength where others can't. I sometimes will bring an individual alongside as I fulfill a leadership duty, giving him a small portion of the responsibility to see how he handles it. It's exciting when that person begins to stretch beyond his comfort zone and he sees the Lord using his meager efforts to impact ministry. Since maturity and skill are developed through experience, I like to "test" some of the men in our church who would never imagine they could serve in a leadership capacity. In fact, very often the best in people emerges when they know they are being counted on for the good of the whole.

WHAT TO LOOK FOR

The truth of the matter is that some men make effective leaders and some do not. Have you ever noticed that there are aspiring leaders whom we know, if given an opportunity, who will abuse the role or be ineffective? I have watched with interest over the years at the tendency of churches, seminaries, Christian colleges and organizations to appoint leaders based on all the wrong qualifications. People are elevated because they are glib, funny, highly organizational, multi-tasking, type-A personalities, or older than everyone else. Many churches find out too late that a leader simply isn't suited for the influential position he's been given. Whether we're talking about elders or under-shepherds in some responsible capacity, failure to carefully assess life patterns *before* appointing men to leadership is disastrous. In their book *The Deliberate Church*, Mark Dever and Paul Alexander offer the following insights:

> By *recognizing* elders before we train them, we're simply acknowledging that a man is already living with elder-quality character and doing elder-type relational work without having the title. By *training* elders before we recognize them as such, we're taking a man who may not have displayed any of these character traits or discipling habits and trying to mold him into a shape he hasn't yet taken. Gathering [leaders] by recognition enables us to spot those men in the congregation who are actually proving by their lifestyle that they are elders in deed, even if not in title. Their actions give evidence that God is raising them up for leadership in the church, and their

selfless concern for the church's corporate life tips us off
that they have an elder's outlook and maturity.[1]

While Dever and Alexander are dealing primarily with the
role of an elder, the principle is sound and works equally well for
cultivating shepherds at any level of ministry. Since developing
leaders from within the local church is essential to her ongoing
strength, finding the right raw materials in people before they are
given responsibility is critical. Premature appointment of leaders can erupt into long-term problems when we're not vigilant (1
Tim 5:24–25). We must look for individuals who already manifest
some basic patterns of life and giftedness in order to cultivate the
most God-honoring leaders. First Timothy 3:1–7 and Titus 1:7–9
are the definitive texts on the character of a spiritual leader in the
church. Young, potential leaders in the body who have not yet
been appointed to spiritual responsibility can begin to cultivate
some of the following foundational qualities in raw form.

FAITHFULNESS IN LITTLE TASKS

The first practical quality I look for in a potential leader is the willingness to give his whole heart to ministry responsibility, no matter how seemingly unimportant. This principle is so often overlooked, leading to the premature elevation of men who are largely
unproven as to their work habits. Yet, the Scriptures put the highest premium on the right motives for our work. Colossians 3:23–
24 says, "Whatever you do, work heartily, as for the Lord and not
for men … . You are serving the Lord Christ." When a young man
asks me about being mentored for leadership in the church, I want
to know where and how he has already been serving. This helps me
know whether he has been faithful *without* title and reputation.
And when I offer a few rather inconsequential responsibilities, I

---

1   Mark Dever and Paul Alexander, *The Deliberate Church: Building Your Ministry on the Gospel*
(Wheaton, IL: Crossway Books, 2005), 138; emphasis original.

look to see if he does his work "heartily," as though he serves only one Master. I've worked with many young men who are enthusiastic about "leading" but give minimal effort when the task is less glamorous. This attitude never works well with greater leadership burdens. Leaders whose "faithfulness" is dependent upon receiving accolades or being recognized as someone to follow will always abuse positions of power when the time comes.

ACCEPTANCE OF RESPONSIBILITY FOR FAILURE

Men who hide weakness and blame others where they are responsible create nothing but trouble for a leadership team. When I survey the men of our church for leadership potential, I look for someone who uses failure as a learning tool, someone who understands that "as long as the grace of God is operative, human failure is never final."[2] When men have a habit of exposing others under their leadership to ridicule in order to appear blameless, they cannot lead the sheep in selfless gospel ministry. If a man is willing to blameshift, he will be prone to dishonesty, especially among other leaders. I have known pastors who simply cannot rest knowing that someone else saw them fail. When a decision falls flat, instead of making careful corrections based on good troubleshooting, their second decision is worse than the first. Failure for them is worse than death; their reputation in the eyes of others is of highest concern. It is also common for such men to chafe at having to seek forgiveness when their failures hurt others. On the other hand, the raw qualities of genuine honesty and teachability accelerate a man's learning and skill. Mistakes are a normal part of spiritual leadership, but greater discernment is forfeited when we're unwilling to own up to them. Look for potential leaders among those who know their need for much learning.

---

2   John MacArthur, "Perfect Love: The Qualities of True Love," Sermon Transcript, http://www.biblebb.com/files/mac/sg1867.htm, (accessed March, 2006).

COMFORTABLE AMONG GIFTED PEERS

When we talk of "team players," the raw quality usually being described is a person who understands where he best fits for achieving the end results. I try to find men who don't see themselves as the answer to every issue. They understand that gifts are distributed "by one and the same Spirit, who apportions to each one individually as he wills" (1 Cor 12:11). Chapter 7 deals extensively with jealousy over giftedness, but the heart of the matter is simply that men must be content with how God determines to use them. Too many elders/pastors waste ministry energies sinfully vying for importance and significance rather than being thankful and content, rejoicing over the gifted leaders around them. Young men with this problem typically have a romanticized view of the ministry. They imagine that being known as the "teacher" or "counselor" adds to their spiritual trophy case, and that real influence somehow comes only from earning a pedestal. If a church appoints a man who has never dealt successfully with this tendency, it will become more difficult for him to acknowledge and overcome. Those men in the church who demonstrate a contentedness—even an overt thankfulness—at the special abilities and effectiveness of others are the ones to pray over, spend time with, mentor, and cultivate into the next generation of leaders.

PATIENT WITH INADEQUACY IN OTHERS

Let's face it: young men struggle more than most with patience. Every new doctrine they learn quickly becomes a bludgeon with which to pound truth into the saints. What's worse, they rarely see their own weaknesses clearly but think they see others with such insight. Add leadership responsibilities to this guy and ministry takes on a whole new flavor. I look for a potential leader who spends most of his time working on his own limitations and gleaning from the skills of others who are more mature. When the sins of fellow believers cause problems, a patient man understands that people need time to develop, that they are the workmanship of Christ (Eph 2:10). A spiritual novice who is critical of others doesn't care that he has weaknesses, but is determined to make his world comfortable by forcing others to shore up theirs. Not a good choice for a leader! An effective leader staffs to his limitations with the skills and gifts of others. He looks to the common good and never places himself where it wouldn't be most beneficial. Look for young men who demonstrate a growing graciousness and forbearance where others make mistakes.

GRACIOUS ACCEPTANCE OF CRITICISM

This quality in its maturity is spelled out thoroughly in Chapter 8, but in its rawest form describes someone who isn't easily offended and sees the value of self-examination (Ps 139:23–24; 1 Cor 13:5). Aspiring young leaders find this most difficult, so when I see this pattern in a potential leader I know they've labored hard in the disciplines of sanctification. They also tend to be very gentle when confronting others, knowing that it is God's grace that keeps them from falling into temptation (Gal 6:1).

PASSION AND OPTIMISM

Leaders cannot compel others to follow or listen unless they passionately believe with full conviction the truth they call others to imbibe. Some men can articulate their beliefs with pinpoint accuracy, but they are so lifeless and joyless that no one dares stay around them for fear of becoming depressed! Serving in the struggle of gospel ministry is always an overwhelming strain to them, the problems of ministry are their greatest frustration, and the fruit of their labor never seems enough to lift their countenance. The problem is that they become cynical about the struggles of leading sheep that need constant care. People-trouble is wearying indeed. It's easy to grow cold and sarcastic about those particularly difficult people whose afflictions are largely self-induced. When a man takes the role of spiritual leader and comes in with selfish expectations, swift discouragement results when they aren't met. The church today calls it "burnout," but in many cases it's a simple matter of wanting ministry to function a certain way and resenting it when it doesn't. Habitual cynics don't make good shepherds. I pray for individuals who look at the church and see not whiners and complainers to be avoided, but broken lives and needy souls who have been purchased by the precious blood of Christ (1 Pet 1:19). Hopeful optimism in ministry is like fresh water in the desert: people's thirst for the tender care of a shepherd is fully satisfied.

TRUST FROM CLOSE FRIENDS

One final raw quality to watch for is a reputation of trustworthiness. Our leadership team is very slow about affirming men to our elder council because of the challenges we would face when someone cannot be trusted. Whether situations involve handling sensitive information, admonishing rebels with skill, coming alongside those who are fainthearted, visiting the infirmed, or accurately handling God's Word, we must be able to trust each other to bring only God's agenda to bear upon the work. If a young potential leader is held at arm's length by those closest to him, or if they doubt the stability of his character, he's not ready. I want to work with men who've earned the confidence of their closest comrades, those who know their personal life, behavior patterns, and consistent choices. No earthly riches are worth the loss of a good name (Prov 22:1). The godly servants of Acts 6:3, appointed to help resolve a serious conflict in the church, were chosen because they were men "of good repute." Everyone knew that these men were absolutely trustworthy! No one even flinched when they were given responsibility over money, food distribution, and proper shepherding of wrong attitudes. These men were known by their friends as having integrity. Paul told Timothy that overseers must also be men who are "well thought of by outsiders" (1 Tim 3:7). When the raw quality of trustworthiness shows up, there is the making of a strong leader.

Lord, the church today starves for men who have the foundational character qualities needed for powerful, lasting leadership. Raise them up in our ministries, Father, and help us to recognize and train them. It's tempting to default to the easy path, giving spiritual responsibility to the unproven and unprepared. We can put a warm body into a slot, but Your people suffer when we get so careless. Help us to keep the standard for godly leadership where You have set it, and may we never secretly wish for shortcuts to the process.

14

SHAPING THE NEXT GENERATION

At the beginning of my ministry, I was already convinced that I needed to pour my life into the men around me. But the church's circumstances at the time made building relationships with the leaders ten times more critical. They had come through a crisis over the previous four years, which began with a moral failure at the very top, sending the fellowship into a long-term upheaval never before encountered by these men. I needed to earn their trust, but it wouldn't come overnight or through surface interaction. We needed a consistent and very concentrated time of prayer, and a focused study on what it means to shepherd the church. We began to meet at 6:00 a.m. on Monday mornings, partly because the schedule of one of our elders prevented him taking a different day, and partly because, in the providence of God, my willingness to meet in the early hours of Monday (after a full Lord's Day) would encourage greater commitment in them. I decided to work through a two-year cycle of teaching, concentrating on every aspect of pastoral theology—practical ministry for spiritual leaders. We called these meetings our "Monday Leadership Training," a kind of leadership practicum and forum for questions and discussions on shepherding issues.

Seventeen years into my ministry in this church, we're still meeting every week, adding new potential leaders by the year.

During the (now) three-year cycle, we cover the following areas of practical ministry:

- Church leadership/shepherding
- Resolving leadership conflicts
- Church government
- Philosophy of ministry (non-negotiables)
- Biblical discipleship/counseling
- Understanding worship and music in the local church
- Church discipline
- Women's role in local church
- Spiritual gifts/body life
- Shepherding families
- Dealing with crises
- Divorce and remarriage
- Studying Scripture (basic hermeneutics)
- Overview of theology
- Teaching Scripture (assigned texts and evaluations)
- Contemporary issues
- Church history

Our prayer times, the challenging implications of each week's study, and the life-on-life interaction as co-laborers has been one of the greatest contributors to the health of our ministry, and without doubt the strongest safeguard against trouble in the leadership. What has made it so effective? Well, for one thing, regularly hearing about the burdens each of us carries and praying for one another's needs works to prevent attitudes of indifference, tendencies toward becoming distant and isolated in self-pity, and being overly distracted and busy—not alert to the struggles of spiritual responsibility. Another reason these times are so powerful is because it is much more difficult to criticize one another when you're together every week laboring in the nuts and bolts of how truth applies to the challenges of ministry. We hear each other's passions, we see the unique gifts, skills, talents, and experience

God has placed on this team, and we come face-to-face with each other's limitations. Tension and strong disagreement among leaders don't have the luxury of festering when we know we're going to pray and study together the following week. Not every relational challenge is absorbed by these strategic training times, but without them our leadership may not have survived even the first few skirmishes after I arrived.

But it's more than just getting together to assimilate information. In fact, spiritual leaders in all kinds of ministries have doctrinal statements and philosophies of ministry that they all affirm. And perhaps they even meet together somewhat regularly to refine their core values and further discuss the programs of the church. Some ministries have turned committee meetings into a science, and the support staff and leadership suffers greatly under an endless array of "informational" meetings where the communication of logistical data and organizational details is the only benefit. You can grow a highly-tuned administrative machine that way, but leadership in these environments will lead to "managing" the ministry rather than leading it. Something else is desperately needed when spiritual leaders gather for discipleship, training, and encouragement. Below are some principles for turning the raw materials of leadership into effective and godly spiritual influencers.

DOCTRINE DERIVED FROM SCRIPTURE

The first priority during these leadership training times is to demonstrate the clarity, power, authority, and sufficiency of God's Word. The team of potential leaders need to hear the truth taught with clarity and precision (2 Tim 2:15); they need to see how the biblical principles for ministry are directly connected to our theology, which is derived from a straightforward, inductive study of Scripture. Decisions regarding the life and direction of the church are not always made with the clearest understanding of the principles behind them. Strong leadership learns how to refine and clearly articulate what it believes and why. Such influence slowly begins to permeate the church, flowing down from the leadership to every area of ministry.

This requires that leaders learn to make their way around their own Bibles. It's sad having to state this at all when it comes to spiritual leadership in the church, but many shepherds and leaders have never been taught Bible knowledge basics, let alone a summary of orthodox doctrine. Training leaders begins with teaching the men theology, both systematic and practical. I'm sure all of us would be shocked to know how little doctrine and theology can be summarized by the average church leader. I've even found elders who can't quickly find their way through the Bible, having never learned the layout of the sixty-six books! They don't know how many historical books there are, how many poetic books, how many prophets wrote. Some spiritual leaders have never read the minor prophets, others can't recall how many epistles Paul wrote, and still others, stunningly, don't consider such knowledge all that important. It's no wonder the sheep are so often lost in a sea of confusion, error, and carnality. How are we going to lead the church if we're not demonstrating that the Word of God is our highest and most sacred trust? With our leaders, early on we study what we call "the non-negotiables of effective gospel ministry," which include a right view of God, the Scriptures, sin, salvation in Christ, the church, and biblical leadership. No matter how you accomplish it, your next generation of leaders must know their Bibles!

CLEAR APPLICATION OF TRUTH

When I was growing up my father used to tell me that if I would immerse myself in the Scriptures I would be wiser than my teachers. It was a strange concept to me at the time, but I have come to understand the reality of his challenge. It was based upon the promises of Psalm 119:97–100:

> Oh how I love your law! It is my meditation all the day.
> Your commandment makes me wiser than my enemies,

for it is ever with me. I have more understanding than all my teachers, for your testimonies are my meditation. I understand more than the aged, for I keep your precepts.

David speaks of the skillful application of truth to one's life. Learning theology alone makes a young man conceited, but submission to the truth in its wise application to life's moral issues—heart and mind stuff—brings wisdom and understanding far beyond the world's most sage counsel.

In our leadership training, we take time to work our theology out in its implications for the inner man (right thinking and believing), and its specific application on a practical level (conformity of actions and life choices). It does us no good to indoctrinate up-and-coming leaders in the truth without giving them the tools for its skillful application. Potential leaders need to see a clear line between conviction and life change. When that line is blurred, leadership becomes guesswork and/or the survival of the strongest opinion. On occasion, I'm asked to meet with an entire elder leadership team of a church. As we talk through the challenges they are facing, it often becomes apparent that there is a disconnect between their stated beliefs and how they actually operate. It's as though the doctrinal statement was completed and uploaded to the website, but everyone defaulted to doing ministry "the way we've always done it." It's quite common these days to peruse church websites, noting the glaring contradictions between their doctrine and the ministries they engage in and support. What we need is to regularly tackle tough issues with our leadership team, immersing ourselves in God's Word and making careful, practical application to every appropriate area.

CONSISTENT PHILOSOPHY OF MINISTRY

As stated above, many leaders can articulate a theological belief, but the ministries of the church do not reflect these same truths as they are fleshed out. Everyone has a philosophy of ministry and lives by it. Unfortunately, many do not know why it is they do what do, nor whether that bears any relationship on their doctrinal beliefs. Aspiring leaders should be required to put feet to their theology in some form of written biblical philosophy of ministry. There are several benefits: (1) it "connects" spiritual service to the authority of Scripture; (2) it unifies each ministry around singular purposes; (3) it prevents involvement in unnecessary distractions that take away from the priorities of the church; (4) it provides clear direction to the leadership of every ministry, from caring for infants to serving the senior saints.

As you develop leaders, take time to write a philosophy of ministry together as the outworking of your church's statement of faith and biblical vision for ministry. Begin with the great commission (Matt 28:19–20), then work through the biblical priorities of the church (Rom 12:1–21; Eph 4:11–16; Col 1:28–29; 1–2 Tim; Titus; Heb 10:24–25; 1 Pet 4:10). Create a basic teaching outline, give it to the church and begin a series of messages on the subject. Using a title like "The Non-Negotiables" was helpful for our people because it is easily recognized by everyone in the ministry. We all know the basic outline of our philosophy of ministry and how it is fleshed out in the life of the body. Leaders who have been grounded in the application of truth and trained to take their theology "to the streets" are the most effective decision-makers, the most discerning counselors, and the most spiritually qualified shepherds.

COURAGE IN CONFLICT

Strength at the leadership level requires spiritual fortitude when it really counts—during significant battles for the souls of men. The absence of good leadership in the church today is the direct result of decades of weak convictions and watered-down doctrine. Aspiring leaders need to know how to take a stand without fear. As we mentor them, we must be "steadfast, immovable, always abounding in the work of the Lord" (1 Cor 15:58), and we must not abdicate our responsibility when trouble comes (John 10:10–13; see Chapter 4).

AVAILABILITY, COMPASSION, AND SACRIFICE

Potential leaders need the constant encouragement of men who will take the time to bring them along. Paul was such a great model, and it is a grace from the Lord that we have so many of his letters that we might see how to train others in the work of the ministry. He served the Ephesian elders "night and day ... with tears" (Acts 20:31, NASB); the weaknesses and struggles of believers became his own as he helped others bear up under trials (2 Cor 11:28–29); he was willing to pour himself out as an act of worship so that others might enjoy strengthened faith and character (Rom 1:11–12; Phil 2:17); his love for his sheep was like that of a tender mother and a truth-loving father (1 Thess 2:7–12); and his encouragement and sacrifice on behalf of his young apprentice, Timothy, became the exclamation point on his leadership! If our men are going to grow as leaders, we must spend time with them. They must see that we're willing to patiently teach, fervently pray, compassionately guide, graciously forgive, humbly walk alongside, and tirelessly sacrifice time, so that they begin to flourish in the role God has called them to fulfill as spiritual leaders.

DISCERNMENT REGARDING "GRAY AREAS"

We would all love for decisions to be more black and white rather than fall into the category of "gray areas." It would be much easier to lead others if we had all the clear answers right at our fingertips, no questions, there it is and that's final! But God, in His infinite wisdom, knows that we would abuse such realities instead of depend upon Him in faith. Life is filled with gray areas so that God's people can live together in harmony while being forced to keep holding "faith and a good conscience" (1 Tim 1:19). All leaders will be somewhat different in where their consciences land

204 COURAGEOUS CHURCHMEN: LEADERS COMPELLING ENOUGH TO FOLLOW

regarding gray areas, but a good leadership team will develop and practice biblical principles for dealing with these areas so that we can help others avoid damaging their conscience or becoming arrogant and self-righteous (Rom 14:1–15:4).

The following is a brief list[1] of helpful questions which promote honest reflection and compel leaders to think biblically and critically not only about each decision but also the motives behind it.

WILL IT BE A SPIRITUAL ADVANTAGE TO MY LIFE?

In other words, will I be enhancing my growth by doing this or that? Will it cultivate more strength, endurance, discipline, and discernment? Will it build rather than tear down my life? Sleep may be a good thing, but too much of it will not be profitable. There's nothing wrong with recreation and leisure, but without careful parameters one could be spiritually weakened (1 Cor 6:12–20; 10:23–31).

WILL IT SLOW ME DOWN WITH EXCESS BAGGAGE IN THE CHRISTIAN RACE?

We are to live our Christian lives by faith. There are certain activities or behaviors which may not be wrong but could become excess distraction and temptation for some. Living a faithful life for the Lord requires diligence, perseverance, struggle, and focus. We should avoid behaviors and activities that add bulk to an already challenging set of spiritual priorities (1 Cor 9:24–27; Heb 12:1–3).

---

1   I am deeply indebted to Dr. John MacArthur for the basic framework and substance of these principles. I learned them early on from his preaching and writing ministries, and I offer them here with adaptations from my own application of his insights. His original message containing these basic principles is entitled "Making the Hard Decisions Easy," http://www.biblebb. com/files/MAC/80-24.htm (accessed July, 2007).

WILL IT POTENTIALLY ENSLAVE ME?

According to God's Word we are not to allow anything to "master" us (1 Cor 6:12, NASB). Whatever your decision about a gray area of life, you must stay away from that thing which will bring you under its power. Because of sinful desires which are *at war* with God's Spirit within us (Jas 4:1), we can easily underestimate the enticement of everyday experiences. Many people have quickly come under the bondage of entertainment, media, food, money, romance and a host of other enjoyments God has richly given to us. We often rationalize by conveniently overestimating our spiritual ability to say no (as in the case of Demas—2 Tim 4:10).

WILL IT HYPOCRITICALLY
COVER MY SINFUL DESIRES?

In other words, am I claiming to do it in the name of true biblical freedom when the truth of the matter is that I'm really satisfying sinful desires? We are to be honest with ourselves. We are not to put a veil over our sinful motives while pretending to be truly "free in Christ" (1 Pet 2:16). It is very common to turn liberty into license (Gal 5:13). If you spend a good bit of time defending your "privilege" to exercise a Christian liberty, perhaps you ought to let go of it for a time as a means of testing your motives. Is it truly a "freedom"? If so, it should be easily dispensed with for the sake of maintaining integrity before the Lord.

WILL IT VIOLATE CHRIST'S
SUPREME RULE IN MY LIFE?

Every believer should be submitting every day to the Lordship of Jesus Christ. However, not everyone agrees on just what the Lord wants. Some are convinced in their conscience that something is wrong, and others have a freedom of conscience to do that same thing. We must ask ourselves, "For me personally, is this something the Lord would be pleased with?" If we have any doubts, we should not do it (Rom 14:20–23). If you believe that the Lord's will for your life would not be violated, then you're free to proceed (Rom 14:5). But be careful here: Paul warns us to be *completely* free from doubts. In other words, we should not be involved in some "gray" activity without having sought counsel, studied God's Word, prayed, and scrutinized all possible pros and cons before proceeding. If important issues are bypassed and the conscience is violated, the result is sin (Rom 14:23).

WILL IT IMPAIR MY JUDGMENT OR HINDER THE HOLY SPIRIT'S CONTROL OF MY WILL?

We are taught by Scripture that we must yield our will to the complete direction of the Holy Spirit (Rom 8:6–14; Gal 5:16–25; Eph 5:18). Any activity that may diminish our ability to remain alert and sensitive to the things of God should not be taken lightly. This principle can have broad and specific application for the Christian. For example, unregulated relationships with unbelievers can cloud one's judgment, plant seeds of confusion about the truth, and desensitize us to the Spirit's conviction (1 Cor 15:33–34). Consider also the very real dangers associated with chemical substances (e.g., pain medication, alcohol, tobacco, etc.), which may lower inhibitions and skew our moral compass. We must be careful to avoid if possible all potential hindrances to the influence of the Holy Spirit.

WILL IT BUILD UP OTHER CHRISTIANS BY ITS EXAMPLE?

We must never exercise a Christian freedom at the expense of another's faith. What you do in front of others is not simply a matter of your freedom in Christ to live as you choose, but rather an issue of building up other believers in their spiritual maturity. We must be careful not to unwittingly encourage another toward a behavior that may violate that person's conscience, thereby putting "a stumbling block or hindrance in the way of a brother"

(Rom 14:13). The pattern of our lives sets an example, and it is a tremendous encouragement to carefully limit our liberty out of love so as to never hurt a brother or sister in the Lord (Rom 14:15; 1 Cor 10:23–33).

WILL IT LEAD OTHERS TOWARD CHRIST?

This is a very difficult issue. The Bible teaches that we are never to get into a situation where our innocent behavior is "spoken of as evil" (Rom 14:16). For example, if what we are doing, though not sinful, could misrepresent the Lord, His church, His people, or His truth, to the world, then we should avoid it. Not only should we build up less mature believers in the body but we should also have character that is above legitimate question in the eyes of unbelievers (1 Pet 2:12–24; 3:13–17; 4:15). Some things are not evil but can easily be associated with questionable elements of society or even worldliness. Remember, if Christian freedoms are truly "freedoms," then we should be as ready and willing to give them up as enjoy them.

WILL IT BE CONSISTENT WITH CHRISTLIKE CHARACTER?

We want to imitate Jesus Christ in all our desires, words, thoughts, and deeds. If we say we belong to Christ, then our first consideration when deciding whether to do this or that should be what the Scriptures teach about our Lord's attitude toward His heavenly Father, toward obedience, toward people, toward the truth, etc. Is this consistent with who He is, His likeness? Could this bring His name and the gospel into question? Will others see what I'm doing and question my commitment to follow Him (1 John 1:6; 2:6)?

WILL IT MAGNIFY THE GLORY OF GOD?

We should live in such a way that the Word of God is honored (Titus 2:5) and God's glory is on display (1 Cor 10:31). We must ask if the activity or behavior could undermine God's name. Could God's honor and praise be diminished as a result of this? Some things may seem mundane and rather non-spiritual (e.g., eating, working with hobbies, leisure, etc.) but Christians must always be alert as to how God can be gratefully praised for all He has provided. We must avoid anything that could detract from bringing Him thankful praise for everything we have the freedom to enjoy.

We must teach our men the skill of applying the above principles in their leadership responsibilities. Beyond these questions, believers have the liberty to make decisions in those areas where the Scriptures give no clear direction for what is sin. Those who are *less free* in their consciences are warned not to judge others who are free, but rather be thankful for God's leading in their life (Rom 14:3b–4). This is very difficult for the "less free" to balance. What their consciences perceive as sinful easily becomes a universal standard for everyone because their conscience is strongly affirmed by strict avoidance of such activities. Consequently, they will feel less fearful and more comfortable when others adhere to the same conduct. However, believers whose consciences are not as "free" as those of others must first acknowledge their internal boundaries and be honest about the tendency to judge others without biblical warrant (Rom 14:3b–13a). They should confess the sin of judging and seek the forgiveness of those whom they have offended. Second, they should thank God for their present state of maturity and for using the conscience to protect them from potential dangers unforeseen. Third, they must press on to maturity in the Scriptures by studying each issue so as to properly inform their conscience along clear, biblical lines. Finally, they should be patient as the Lord works in their hearts to cultivate discernment and balance, never violating their spiritual sensibilities in the meantime.

Regarding those with *greater liberty*, Romans 14:13b–21 and 15:1 warn them not to think less of others without freedom, but rather love them by first never being an offense or spiritual hindrance. Wherever a complaint arises, careful and thoughtful interaction should follow so that an understanding is reached for God's glory. The conscience of one should not rule another in areas of liberty, but love should prevail in every consideration, even if it means eliminating the exercise of certain liberties (e.g., Paul in 1 Cor 8:12–13). Second, serious consideration should be given to whether a liberty is the best choice in a particular context. Some Christian freedoms may be unquestioned because of cultural norms or common Christian practice, while the freedom in other contexts may be imprudent because of the spiritual background and history of certain groups and peoples. For example, the mealtime consumption of wine may be the norm and so one's liberty (all other spiritual questions above having been considered) will most likely be a non-issue. On the other hand, in a culture where the abuses of alcohol are decried by both the saved and the unsaved, such liberty may cause greater questions and bring an unintended but very real reproach upon Christ and His church.

Finally, those with greater liberty of conscience should carefully discern the difference between a "clear" conscience and a "seared" one. Some participate in "gray" activities with ease because they have consistently and with cavalier involvement suppressed the warnings of their conscience. This is often rationalized by appealing to the absence of an explicit text prohibiting the practice. How can we know the difference? According to 1 Timothy 1:5–7, when the conscience is silenced, the result is "vain discussion"(fruitless and senseless talk), pride, and arrogant but ignorant assertions about truth (see also 1 Tim 4:2–3). In other words, the more people engage in activities which their consciences warn them against, the more they become blinded to the truth, cannot see the dangers, and therefore, perceive themselves to be "free," though they are deceived. Conversely, the evidence of a clear and maturing conscience is simply humility, submissiveness, and obedience (1 Pet 2:16–19; 3:16–17). Where these are absent it is a given that one's conscience may "feel" free but is simply suppressed. In conclusion, Paul spoke of each of these realities within the church, and we should not be surprised at the struggle. Remember, we shall all give an account of ourselves before God (Rom 14:10)!

One of the most excited aspects of training men in the local church is that God uses that process to stir the hearts of those He is calling to serve the church as shepherds of His flock. Pastoral training in the context of the local church has fallen on hard times. The formal side of theological education has been outsourced to institutions of higher learning. The church has benefitted from the ability to send one of their own to a seminary where the concentrated study environment puts the student through the theological and ministry paces and affirms his gifts and skills with God's Word. Unfortunately, over the years the church has been viewed as completely unable to provide theological training at the seminary level. And churches have largely capitulated to this model, backing away from pastoral training altogether. I believe that the church can and should train men, theologically and pastorally, right in the context of the local church. I believe it is the ideal model for the training and sending of pastors.

CHURCHMEN TRAINING CHURCHMEN

With centuries of tradition we've grown accustomed to the institutional model of seminary training. But the longer I've shepherded the flock of God, the more persuaded I've become that churchmen should train churchmen. History has proven that the truth isn't safe in the institution. Scripture declares, however, that "the pillar and support of the truth" is "the church of the living God" (1 Tim 3:15, NASB). The seedbed of churchmen is the church!

Paul's 2 Timothy 2:2 mandate to make replicating disciples is a pastoral charge. It doesn't allow for discipleship in the life of the church to be stripped away from the academic component. The institutional model of seminary training is foreign to the 2 Timothy 2:2 mandate. It is the responsibility of shepherds in the church to train its future shepherds.

With over a decade of training churchmen at The Expositors Seminary, I have the profound privilege of laboring alongside fellow shepherds in the trenches as we train men for ministry. The four-year

Master of Divinity curriculum is integrated with hands-on learning of ministry skills in the context of the local church. As the course catalog attests, the formal instruction emphasizes the indispensables of the biblical languages, expository preaching, exegetically-derived theology, and shepherding. This intensive coursework combines with in-the-field experience for robust, real-world training.

In the first year we focus on mentorship as shepherds get to know new students to decide which areas of ministry they should get involved with. In this mentorship process we look for areas of giftedness and areas to grow, and we watch for patterns of ambition and idols of personal significance. Progressing into his second year, the shepherd-in-training receives increased exposure to the demands of church ministry where the rigors of the classroom run side by side with his education "in the field." In this apprenticeship He serves practical needs, sits in on leadership meetings, goes along on visitation, observes counseling as appropriate, and teaches as assigned by leadership. These contexts provide opportunities to evaluate his strengths and weaknesses, and to identify mistakes. The third year begins an internship where the pastoral student is challenged further as he takes on more leadership and begins to compose correspondence addressing ministry issues, counseling concerns, and theological questions. The fourth year of preparation culminates in a pastoral residency designed to provide the highest level of supervised ministry experience. Close-range shepherding and practicum are built into the fabric of the training environment. The pastor-professors at The Expositors Seminary are in the practice of drawing in men for ministry opportunities and evaluation.

The early days of Princeton Seminary was a time when apprenticeship was inseparable from scholarship. After Archibald Alexander was chosen by the church to be Princeton Seminary's first professor in 1812, he began meeting with

> his little class of three students once a day. They worked their way through a long list of subjects which included

Hebrew, Old Testament, Bible history and geography, Greek, and English Bible. Six more students arrived by the next spring, and another five joined the first-year class in the summer. Alexander's modest home was the library, chapel, and classroom. The students studied there and shared meals and family worship.[2]

Shepherds shoulder the responsibility to train up faithful men. Because of the sobering weight of ministry leadership, we foster a setting where men are taught to get in the flow of discipleship, to humbly submit to the elders, and to joyfully serve wherever there is a need—without regard for being noticed or being obscure. By so doing we protect the flock of God from the spiritual vulnerability that comes with unprepared shepherds—and we protect the pastoral student from his own inclination toward self-significance. Apart from the sobering demands of church ministry and the accountability of close-range oversight, shepherds-in-training tend to lose sight of the call of Scripture to shepherd the flock of God with eagerness and humility as we anticipate the appearing of our Chief Shepherd, Jesus Christ (1 Pet 5:1–4)!

> *Dear Lord Jesus, Your church needs a generation of leaders who are grounded in truth, living in holiness, and shepherding the flock with wisdom and skill. Be merciful to our churches as we strive to mentor and train the next generation of spiritual leaders. Forgive us for neglect, fear of man, hypocrisy, and lack of conviction. Make us, by Your Spirit, to stand in the evil day, being saturated with divine truth and submissive to its power. Amen.*

---

2   David B. Calhoun, *Princeton Seminary*, vol. 1, *Faith and Learning 1812–1868* (Carlisle, PA: The Banner of Truth Trust, 1994), 59.

CONCLUSION

What, then, is leadership? It is the God-given ability to influence others through the power of a godly life and the wisdom gained in the practice of truth. God's people are suffering greatly today for lack of dynamic spiritual influence. Oh, there are all kinds of influence being had—popularity contests, business savvy, political power, financial manipulation, social mobilization, etc.—and such methods have infiltrated the work of the church, captivating the affections of her leaders who seem ready to chase every new fad on the horizon. These tactics are impotent when it comes to true leadership. Leading others to real change and spiritual growth demands character that has walked that same path in victory. We must abandon the pop-techniques of the business world and the communal overtones of the postmodern, anti-authority bent. As the spiritual leaders of today who are teaching those of tomorrow, we must be able to articulate the truth with piercing clarity, our lives must reflect a sober-mindedness and the pursuit of holy living, we must flee from the weaknesses and sinful habits that destroy integrity, faithfulness, and humble obedience, and we must pour our lives into the next generation of God's men. If we bail on this vital responsibility, the people of God will have to live with the fallout. The mandate is clear; our orders are unambiguous. In the words of Paul, "What you have heard from me in the presence of many witnesses entrust to faithful men who will be able to teach others also" (2 Tim 2:2).

BIOGRAPHY

Jerry Wragg has served as Senior Pastor at Grace Immanuel Bible Church in Jupiter, Florida, since 2001. Prior to his ministry in Florida, Jerry served for ten years as Senior Associate Pastor and Personal Assistant to Dr. John MacArthur at Grace Community Church, Sun Valley, California. He serves as President and faculty member of The Expositors Seminary in Jupiter, where he teaches hermeneutics, homiletics, pastoral theology, and contemporary theological issues. He and his wife, Louise, have been married for nearly forty years and have the joy of influencing their eleven grandchildren.

Made in the USA
Monee, IL
08 May 2023

33345327R00128